Easy, Elegant
PUNCHNEEDLE

Easy, Elegant
PUNCHNEEDLE

MARINDA STEWART

STACKPOLE
BOOKS

Copyright © 2013 by Stackpole Books

Published by
STACKPOLE BOOKS
5067 Ritter Road
Mechanicsburg, PA 17055
www.stackpolebooks.com

Printed in U.S.A.

10 9 8 7 6 5 4 3 2 1

First edition

Cover design by Caroline S. Stover
Photographs by Alan Wycheck

Library of Congress Cataloging-in-Publication Data

Stewart, Marinda.
    Easy, elegant punchneedle / Marinda Stewart. — First edition.
      pages   cm
     ISBN 978-0-8117-1226-2
     1. Embroidery—Patterns.   2. Punched work.   I. Title.
TT771.S725   2013
746.44—dc23
                                          2013020392

Contents

Introduction

When I finished writing *Punchneedle: The Complete Guide,* an extensive book on punchneedle embroidery, I thought I'd said everything there was to say. I should have known better.

As I was finishing that book, I began to wonder: What would happen if . . . Could I make punchneedle three-dimensional? I began experimenting, starting with flowers, leaves, and butterflies. I was loosely inspired by traditional stump work, a process of adding dimensional stitched elements to flat embroidery. I wanted my punchneedle to be completely free of any background. Once the kinks were ironed out, I sent a small stemmed flower to Debra Smith, editor of *Rug Hooking* magazine. That tiny flower led to this book.

It's been exciting to create a new body of work to share with other punchneedle enthusiasts. My first book was an encyclopedia of information with very few projects; this book is nearly all projects and half of them are three-dimensional. I've focused on using the most delicate and refined elements of punchneedle to achieve detail and realism. All of the work in this book is worked with one to three strands of six-strand floss. Although these pieces look complicated and time-consuming, they are surprisingly easy and quick to make. However, making seventeen assorted life-sized pansies was a labor of love! The finished result was worth the effort, though. Most of the projects I've designed for this book are small. They are quick and easy, as well as economical, to make. They're fabulous to own or to wear and even better to give as a gift. Most people can't figure out how punchneedle embroidery is done and are amazed at its beauty.

I hope you find something to excite and inspire you in this book. Maybe you'll find the perfect project to give to a loved one or to decorate a bare spot in your house; maybe you'll learn a new trick or pick up a tip to incorporate into your work. If this happens, I'm thrilled. That's the best possible result.

Happy stitching!
Marinda

PART I

Background

CHAPTER I
A Brief History

Punchneedle embroidery is a unique technique for forming many tiny loops of thread to create a design. The technique has been around for several hundred years, to the best of our knowledge. Most current historical information has been pieced together from fragments of oral records along with bits and pieces of embroidered examples.

The examples of punchneedle-style embroidery that have been found span hundreds of years and a number of diverse cultures around the world. This kind of embroidery has been found in the work of nuns in French convents of the 1600s; researchers have proposed that the nuns made their tools from tiny, hollow bird bones. Russian Old Believers, a small religious sect, have embellished their clothing, religious icons, and some household items with punchneedle embroidery since the eighteenth century. There are contemporary Indian and Chinese

Vintage pansy pillow cover.

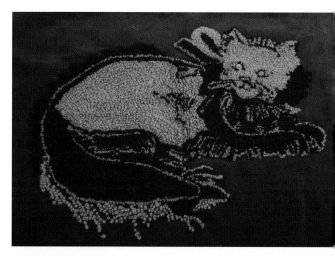

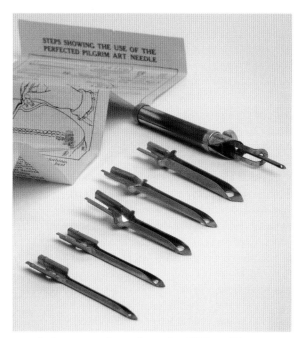

A vintage needle set from the 1920s or 30s.

punchneedle interpretations as well. Unfortunately, we may never know the exact origin of the craft.

In the late 1920s and into the 1930s, punchneedle embroidery was very popular in the United States. Sets of different-sized needles with a common handle were readily available. None of the work was as delicate and refined as can be created with today's needles, but the process was the same.

The cat pillow pictured here dates from this period. The wool punchneedle embroidery was worked on a cotton velveteen background. The eyes are old shoe buttons, giving the cat such a strange look. The pattern was a commercial design printed on gauzy muslin, which was basted on the back of the velveteen. The punchneedle embroidery was worked through both layers.

Whenever I get a chance to go antiquing, I'm always on the lookout for embroidery to add to my collection. I've found World War II pieces from occupied Japan and partially worked embroideries with the loops cut off to give the appearance of vel-

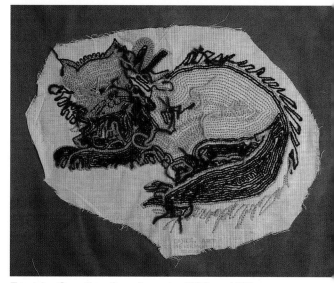

Top right: Cat pillow front from the 1920s to 1930s. Design from Carol Art, Newark, New Jersey.
Above: Back of cat pillow.

vet. I've even come across work which looks like punchneedle but is not, like the flowers on the quilt blocks pictured on page 4. These flowers were made by hand sewing wool yarn on a fine wool fabric and then clipping the strands to make a dense fringe, similar to how you make a pom-pom. The technique is said to have originated in France.

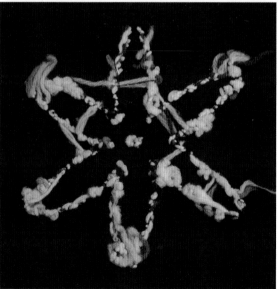

Wool quilt blocks resembling punchneedle embroidery.

Despite being used in many different regions and periods in history, punchneedle embroidery fell out of favor in the 1950s and 60s. As the popularity of other needlecrafts grew, enthusiasm for punchneedle waned until few people remembered it.

The craft survived to make a later resurgence thanks to communities of Russian Old Believers. An offshoot of the Russian Orthodox church that scattered to form small, isolated communities in response to persecution, Russian Old Believers have preserved many aspects of a traditional eighteenth-century lifestyle, including the technique of *igolochkoy* (ego-luch-koy). *Igolochkoy*, which translates to "with a little needle," is a form of punchneedle embroidery which Russian Old Believers use to decorate clothing, religious items, and household objects.

In the 1970s, several "outsiders" were introduced to various Old Believer communities, and through them this special form of punchneedle embroidery was rediscovered. One of these outsiders, Jean Cook Anderson, worked with her new Old Believer friends to start a business teaching the embroidery and selling the tools. It was through Jean that I was first introduced to punchneedle and first saw the incredible detail possible with this type of embroidery. My first punchneedle was an Old Believer tool that held only one strand of embroidery floss—the only size of needle available at the time. One-strand work is exquisite; the detail you can achieve is amazing. This is still my favorite needle size when I'm working on an intricate design.

As the popularity of the craft grew, demand for tools outgrew the Old Believers' production capabilities, and other companies began producing punchneedles. Today, you can buy needles in several different sizes from a number of companies (see the Resources section for more details on where to buy punchneedles).

Today, punchneedle is alive and well, and its popularity has spread to many parts of the world.

Above left: Close-up of iris fan. *Above right:* Chinese punchneedle pillow cover with stylized pansies. *Left:* My original punchneedle, slightly over 1 inch long.

I recently found a contemporary example of commercially produced punchneedle from China, demonstrating the wide range of the craft. This piece was worked with multiple strands of rayon thread in a large needle (#6 or larger). The entire 16" square pillow is covered in embroidery. The design is simple, but it's an interesting piece.

When I first learned punchneedle embroidery I thought it was a novelty. Who knew where it would lead! It's as close to painting with thread as I have ever found, and the more I do it, the more ideas I have for using it in new projects. Historical examples of punchneedle and traditional embroidery continue to inspire me, but I love to combine the craft with other techniques, as you will see in several of the projects in part II of this book.

CHAPTER 2
Tools and Materials

Before you begin doing punchneedle embroidery, you'll need to assemble the proper tools and accessories. There are some basic supplies you'll need for all your punchneedle projects, as well as specialty supplies needed to create some of the specific pieces in this book. I suggest you choose the best products available. The quality of your tools affects the quality of the finished project—and it is easier to work with high-quality tools.

Essential Supplies

First of all, you need a punchneedle or two. All of the projects in this book use either a #1 punchneedle or a #3 or #2/3 punchneedle. The number refers to the number of strands of six-strand embroidery floss the needle will hold. A #1 needle will hold a single strand separated out of the six strands. A #3 punchneedle will hold two or three strands and a #6 needle will use four to six strands of embroidery floss. Some punchneedle manufacturers make individual needles for each size, others have different sized needle tips which fit into a common handle. Needle suppliers are listed in the resouces section at the back of the book. Although I worked a number of the projects in this book with a #1 needle, they can all be worked with two strands of floss in a #3 needle. However, the delicate detail of the embroidery will be reduced with the larger loops.

A necessary feature on any punchneedle is the ability to shorten or lengthen the height of the loops made when stitching. The shorter the loop,

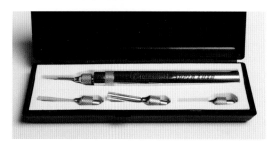

Top to bottom: Set of four needles from Bernadine's Needle Art; set of three needles from Igolochkoy (note the magnetic strip in the lid of the case for holding threaders); Luxo brand punchneedle with interchangeable tips; Ultra Punch needle with tips.

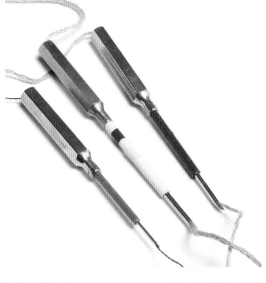

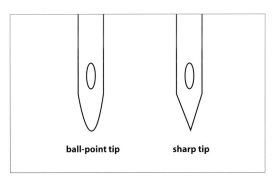

ball-point tip   sharp tip

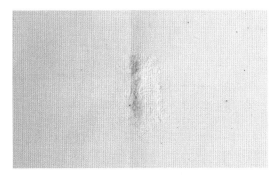

the finer the detail you can achieve. Longer loops can be used for contrast, or the tops can be cut off to make a velvet texture. Both of these techniques are used in some of the projects in this book. The gauge or stopper on the punchneedle determines the loop height. The directions included with your needle are a valuable source of information: Make sure you read them and understand the procedures described, including how to set the loop height and how to thread the needle. Each manufacturer is the ultimate authority on their product.

Before you change the position of the gauge or stopper, measure and record its original position. This is the standard setting and you will need it as a baseline to return to. Every time you adjust your punchneedle to create longer loops for a particular part of a project, be sure to remember to return the gauge or stopper to its original setting, ready to embroider loops of the standard height again.

Purchase the best needle possible. Here's what to look for: The point of the punchneedle should be like a ball-point sewing needle. It will push through the weave but leave it intact. If the needle tip is too sharp, it will tear through the weave, cutting or damaging the fabric; this can cause the loops to be inconsistent or not hold at all. The inside and outside of the needle should be smooth and highly polished, and the thread should flow easily through it. The eye and beveled edge (openings) of the needle should also be smooth, with no rough edges to cut or shred the thread. The eye should be centered in the needle shaft. All of these features ensure even and consistent loops. If the results from your needle are disappointing, consider upgrading to something better—it really does make a difference!

Top to bottom: Threaded needles (left to right): #1, #3, and #6; sample stitches from different-sized needles with longer loops shown on left and shorter loops on right (top to bottom): #1, #3, #6; ball-point tip vs. sharp tip; detail of fabric damaged by embroidery with a sharp-tipped punchneedle.

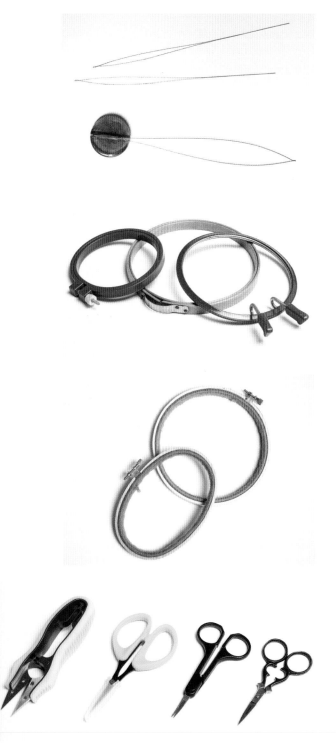

Every needle comes with a threader. There are two types of threaders: double ended and tab ended. The threader that came with your punchneedle will be the best type for that particular needle; specific instructions for threading your needle will be included when you purchase it. I always keep extra threaders on hand, as they are fragile and will eventually bend, kink, break, or disappear.

TIP » Double-ended threaders are especially easy to lose or misplace; they are so thin and fine that they are almost invisible. I protect my threaders (and my sanity) by storing them in a long clear tube with a lid or in a box with a magnetic strip.

Another necessary item is a good wooden embroidery hoop that adjusts with a screw on the outer ring. The screw needs to be long enough to accommodate extra bulk. Spring and tension hoops cannot be adjusted and are not very good for punchneedle. To get good quality stitches, you must be able to stretch the fabric tautly in the hoop.

Certain kinds of hoops can damage your embroidery if they are tightened over a worked area; this can create a "hoop ring" of crushed loops. The best way to prevent this is to use a hoop that is larger than the area you are embroidering. If this is not possible—as for very large projects—the best hoop choice is a padded wooden hoop. I wrap the inner rings of all my hoops with wool or acrylic yarn to protect my work. Plastic hoops are not recommended, as they are more likely to damage punchneedle embroidery. I have an assortment of sizes and shapes of hoops to use for different projects.

As with any kind of embroidery, punchneedle requires a good, small, sharp pair of embroidery scissors. Tiny sharp blades make trimming threads, clipping loops, and cleaning up designs much easier. I have several different small pairs of scissors.

Next, we need thread. All of the projects in this book use six-strand cotton embroidery floss. I've

Top to bottom: Double-ended and tab-ended threaders; spring and tension hoops (not adjustable and therefore poor choices for punchneedle embroidery); wooden hoops padded with yarn to protect embroidery; assorted scissors.

used a Spanish brand called Presencia, along with some boutique over-dyed thread from Weeks Dye Works. The conversion chart included at the back of the book shows you the equivalents for other common brands of floss. Hand-dyed colors don't have any equivalents; they are special unto themselves. I've opted to use the realistic colors found in nature for most of the projects, but you should feel free to change the colors to suit your personal taste.

Finally, we need fabric. The specific fabrics needed are listed for each project in the book. Most of them are quality cottons—the kind found in a good fabric store. Generally speaking, you need a tightly woven fabric so the loops will stay in place. Most often, 100% cotton fabric or a cotton-polyester blend, such as Weaver's Cloth, will be used. Two of the projects in this book use different kinds of silk

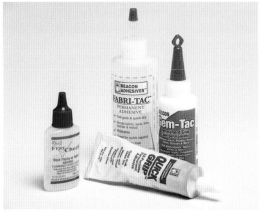

for the backgrounds; another uses a vintage quilt block, probably made of fine wool. Different or unusual fabrics may require special handling; you'll find tips for working with these fabrics in the directions for each specific project.

My favorite background fabric for three-dimensional punchneedle pieces is Cotton Couture, made by Michael Miller Fabrics. This cotton fabric comes in many colors and has a high thread count which gives it the stability necessary for three-dimensional punchneedle pieces.

If you have questions about a particular fabric's suitability, see *Punchneedle: The Complete Guide* for specific recommendations.

Accessories for Particular Projects

Many of the projects in this book will require other miscellaneous items for finishing.

Glue is an essential for many of the projects in this book—and you'll need several different kinds for different purposes. Pay careful attention to which kind of glue is specified in the instructions for each project; different kinds and brands of glue are not interchangeable. Make sure whatever glue you use is flexible when dry; for projects you plan to wash, all glue should be waterproof as well.

First, you'll need a good general all-purpose glue—I use Quick Grip from Beacon Adhesives. Quick Grip is excellent for attaching metal to metal and for mixed medium surfaces.

You'll also need an embellishing glue for securing the embroidery stitches on the backs of your three-dimensional pieces and for attaching jewels and other embellishments. I recommend Gem-Tac embellishing glue from Beacon Adhesives, which contracts as it dries, holding the stitches more securely.

For the three-dimensional projects, you'll also need a seam sealant to keep your base fabric from unraveling when you cut out the pieces; for this purpose, I use Fray-Check from Prym-Dritz.

Top: Assorted 6-strand embroidery floss. *Bottom:* Different glues have different properties and functions. Make sure you use the best one for each step in the process.

Finally, for some projects you will need a good fabric glue such as Fabri-Tac (from Beacon Adhesives).

The products mentioned here give me consistent, predictable results without any problems. If you need to substitute a different glue, work a test sample first. Not all glues will give the same results.

For the three-dimensional projects, I use floral wire to allow me to shape the pieces. I use 32-gauge white cotton-covered floral wire (which I color by hand to match the project) for petals and butterfly wings and 20- and 28-gauge green floral wire for stems and leaves. I like to buy the wire on a spool because there is less waste, but precut lengths also work.

There are a number of ways to hand color the wire to match your project: You can color the wire with a permanent marker, paint it with diluted acrylic paint, rub it on a colored stamp pad, or spray it with floral spray paint. The spray is the messiest and my least favorite; markers and paint are better coloring options.

You'll need green floral tape to attach the wired petals and leaves together and add stems. For many of the projects, you'll also need premade flower stamens; you can find these in the floral or bridal sections of craft stores. In addition to scissors, you'll need needle-nose pliers, wire cutters, tweezers, and clothespins—all useful for projects involving wire.

You'll also need tools and supplies for transferring patterns to the fabric you're going to embroider. Collect a regular pencil, a washable fabric pen, an iron-on transfer pencil, a white or silver fabric pencil (for dark fabrics), dressmaker's carbon paper, and white nylon tricot iron-on interfacing; these items will cover almost every method of

Top to bottom: Cotton-covered floral wire; stamp pads and paintbrush for coloring wire; assorted stamens and floral tape; tools—tweezers, needle-nose pliers, wire cutters, and a clothespin or two.

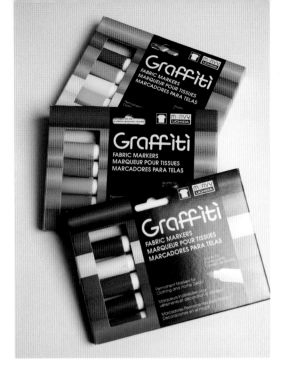

getting a design onto fabric. A light box is nice to have, but you can substitute a window or lighted lampshade. If I am going to use a pattern over and over, as with petals and leaves, I will make a copy out of template plastic. I label each piece and keep them together in a small plastic bag labeled with the project name.

Other projects use miscellaneous extra items such as jewelry findings (earring backs, acrylic jewels, bolo tie tips, and charms), felt, beads, and cardboard or foam-core board. These extra items will be listed in the materials list for each project.

Having a tool or product which gives good, consistent, predictable results makes creating easier and more fun, so invest in the best whenever possible. It is also more fun to create when you have everything you need on hand in a convenient space. If a dedicated workspace is not available, store all your supplies together in one storage container, labeled and easy to get to. My punchneedles live in my repurposed jewelry box, threads are stored in two drawers of a chest, and so on. I get more done if I don't have to find everything first.

Left column, top to bottom: Colored fabric marking pens; dressmaker's carbon paper and iron-on transfer pencils; miscellaneous findings. *Right:* Flat-backed acrylic jewels and assorted sew-on beads.

CHAPTER 3
Basic Techniques

Now the fun begins—learning how to do punch-needle embroidery. It may take a little practice to get comfortable with the needle, achieve even and consistent loops, and develop a rhythm, but once you get the hang of it, everything is easy. Work slowly and deliberately until you are accustomed to the process. Uniformity is more important than speed. Because many of the projects in this book are small, they are easily portable and doable in a few days, so don't be afraid to take your time!

Embroidery Designs

Before you start stitching, you need to select a design. Embroidery designs are available in many different styles and formats.

Commercially available iron-on embroidery transfers are particularly easy to use. Remember to put the transfer facedown on the *back* of the fabric. If there are any letters, words, or numbers in the design, they will need to be reversed so they don't show up backwards on the finished piece. It's a good idea to test the transfer out on a small piece of the same fabric you plan to use for the background. This way you can learn how much heat to use, how long the iron needs to be held in place, and what the quality of the finished transfer will be before committing to the actual project. Most commercial transfers will have a test section and will indicate if they are reusable.

Commercial iron-on transfers.

Fronts and backs of printed fabrics. Notice how the pattern is fainter, but still readable, on the reverse side.

Another easy approach to design is to embroider on already-printed fabric. A number of projects in this book use printed fabric for their designs. With colored fabric, I generally choose threads to match the colors in the background fabric; with one of the black-and-white prints in this book, I used it like a coloring book, picking my own colors to fill in the design. Either way works. It is important the main elements in the design be visible on the wrong side of the fabric, because this will be your pattern. Clean, simple designs are easier to use if you're just starting out.

Transfer Methods

Sometimes there isn't an iron-on transfer or a printed fabric with the design you want. Other times you have a pattern on fabric but the design would be better on a different kind of fabric or a different colored background. In cases like these, you'll need to transfer your chosen design. There are several different methods you can use, depending on the situation.

PATTERNS AND COPYRIGHT

Always make sure you are legally allowed to use the pattern you've selected. Many embroidery designs are copyright free; this means they are in the public domain and do not require permission to be used. Often, designs and patterns are copyrighted but the purchaser may use them for a personal project. This is implied with most patterns that you purchase.

If your design comes from another source or a different medium (such as a photograph, a piece of original artwork, or an illustration in a magazine), you need to get written permission from whoever owns the copyright to the source before you use the design in any way—even if you are altering aspects of the design.

Copyright can be confusing; if you're in doubt, the best advice is to choose something else. This is especially important if you want to exhibit your embroidery in a show or competition. Magazines and contests often will not accept a project from a copyrighted source other than the maker, and individuals who violate copyright can be prosecuted. Better safe than sorry!

Method #1

You can use a light box or window to trace the design directly onto the fabric. Put the design behind the fabric and the light shining through will allow you to trace the design directly onto the back of the fabric. I usually use a fine, regular lead pencil for this method. A wash-out fabric marking pen will also work.

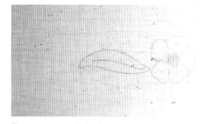

Pattern on a light box.

Method #2

You can also use dressmaker's carbon paper to transfer designs. Place the paper facedown on the fabric, then place the design on top. Trace the design firmly with a stylus, an empty ball-point pen, or a rounded pencil tip. The carbon paper will transfer the design to the fabric. This method will work for light-colored fabric with dark dressmaker's carbon paper, or for dark fabric with light or white dressmaker's carbon paper. The image produced with this method is often faint and may need touching up when you embroider. Do not use office-type carbon paper; it is not designed for use with fabric.

Dressmaker's carbon paper is reusable.

Method #3

You can make your own iron-on transfer using a special iron-on transfer pencil. These pencils are frequently made with a wax base, and generally are available in blue or red. Test the red before using; it can bleed and the lines can be difficult to cover up. There are also white iron-on transfer pens for use on dark fabrics; however, the tips are quite broad so it's hard to achieve delicate detail with them.

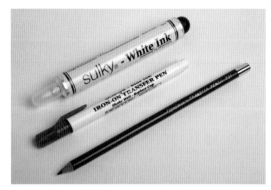

Iron-on transfer pens and pencils.

Follow the pencil manufacturer's directions for creating the transfer and ironing it onto the back of the fabric. I use regular tracing paper to create my design and make my iron-on transfer.

Method #4

Another iron-on method uses nylon tricot fusible interfacing to transfer the design. This method is great for dark fabric because the tricot is white, and for silk, which can't take the heat needed for most iron-on transfers. I used this method for several of the projects in this book, including the vintage pieced quilt block (see page 76), where it solved the problem of dealing with the seams in the piecework. Fuse the interfacing onto the back of the fabric, following the manufacturer's directions, then proceed to transfer your design onto the tricot.

The drawback to this method is that it adds layers of product to work through—the tricot and a layer of glue (the fusible element) in addition to the background fabric. While this can stabilize and strengthen a delicate fabric such as silk and help loops stay in better in a looser fabric like wool, the extra components also make it harder to punch and reduce the natural elasticity of the fabric. Sometimes, though, it's the lesser of two evils.

There are several brands of interfacing available, and they come in white, black, and sometimes nude or beige. I use white, which allows my iron-on transfers to show up more quickly with less heat needed. Less heat also means a reduced possibility of scorching or damaging the base fabric.

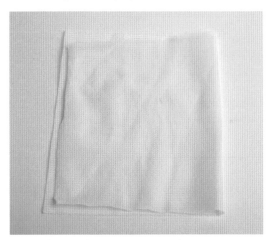

Fusible (iron-on) nylon tricot interfacing.

Method #5

When all else fails, draw the design freehand on the fabric. This works equally well with light and dark fabrics. I use a white or silver fabric pencil on darks and a regular pencil on light fabrics.

When embroidering any design—no matter how you transferred it—make sure you cover any and all pattern lines. This guarantees there will be no nasty design shadow on the front of the embroidery.

Freehand drawing on fabric.

Preparing the Thread

Students frequently ask me, "How long should I cut the thread?" Actually, you can use almost any length. Unlike traditional embroidery done with a hand-sewing needle, punchneedle embroidery uses the part of the thread closest to the needle for each stitch—not the end closest to the knot. The thread is always fresh because it hasn't been pulled through the fabric time and time again. Because of this, you could, theoretically, use an endless piece of thread.

When I use thread on a spool, I don't cut it; it is fed directly off the spool as needed. When working with stranded floss, I cut the longest length I can comfortably manage. If I have to separate strands of floss or blend thread, I rarely use anything longer than a yard; longer pieces get tangled too easily.

Separating out a single strand of six-strand embroidery floss can be a headache—unless you know this easy method: Pinch one end of the cut length of stranded floss, and select a single thread or strand. Still pinching the remaining strands, gently pull the single thread out. The other threads will gather below the pinched area. This method eliminates tangles almost completely. If I'm using multiple threads of a single color, I'll pull each strand out separately and put them back together to stitch.

Threading the Needle

Before you start stitching, you need to thread your needle. Each needle manufacturer includes threading instructions with their needles. Read and follow these directions.

Keep track of the needle threaders for your needle. They are often fragile and can easily be bent, kinked, broken, or lost. It's a good idea to have extras on hand.

Be sure to finish the threading by passing the thread through the eye. If the eye isn't threaded, the needle will not form loops in the fabric. Everyone forgets to do this at least once; I did it just the other day!

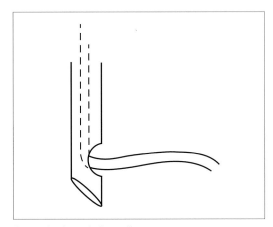

Properly threaded needle.

Leave a scant inch of thread as a tail when you start to stitch. There is no knotting in punchneedle. After making a few stitches to anchor the thread, clip off the tail even with the back of the fabric.

Beginning to Stitch

Once the needle is threaded, you're ready to stitch. Push the needle through the fabric from the back until the gauge or stopper on the shaft stops it. Then pull the needle out *just* to the surface. You'll have left behind a loop on the front of the fabric. Slide or drag the tip across the fabric to where you want to make your next loop and push it back in. And then repeat this process again and again. With each punch, a loop is made on the right side of the fabric. Make sure the thread is flowing evenly through the needle; it is this even flow of thread that creates the loops that make up the design.

Back and front of punchneedle embroidery (enlarged to show detail).

If you have a large or complicated design, it may be a little daunting figuring out where to start. Start by outlining the design with a darker thread, usually the darkest shade of the fill-in color. This helps define the design and gives it a crisp finish. Outline first, work the details within the shape with the same dark shade, then fill in with the main color.

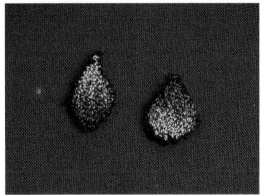

Shaded petals on the stitched side *(top photo)* and the front *(bottom photo)*.

It's important to work in a well-lit, comfortable place. Your light should come from the opposite direction from your stitching hand. I'm right-handed, so my light source is on my left. This lights up my work area and reduces shadows. Sit in a comfortable chair with good support for your back. Don't work too long in one position without getting up to move and stretch. It's good to give your eyes a rest, too. When I'm marathon stitching, I'll set a cooking timer for 45 minutes to an hour to remind myself to move. It's silly but effective.

If you make a mistake or don't like the look of a section, you can pull the loops out and reposition them. However, if you do this, it is best not to use the same thread more than two or three times. Thread that is pulled in and out of the cloth over

and over begins to lose its luster and natural twist. Thread is inexpensive, so don't compromise your finished project by being too frugal. Cut off the used thread and start fresh.

After I work a design, I like to clean it up by re-arranging some of the loops on the front. With the tip of my needle or embroidery scissors, I *carefully* push the loops into place to straighten out detail lines, outlines, and any other places which need some attention. At the same time, I trim any long tag ends or loops even with the surrounding loops. It's amazing how much difference this step makes in the overall appearance of the finished piece. It's certainly worth the trouble. When you finish a piece, take the time to sign and date it somewhere. It's a pity when we lose the identity of the maker of a beautiful piece of embroidery over the years.

Stitching Tips

When you stitch, you should hold the needle at a comfortable angle, around 60 to 70 degrees. It needs to be a little more vertical than the way you would hold a pen or pencil. This keeps your work crisp and clean, with the loops vertical and separate from each other. If you put the needle in at a sharp angle, the new loops will get tangled up with existing loops.

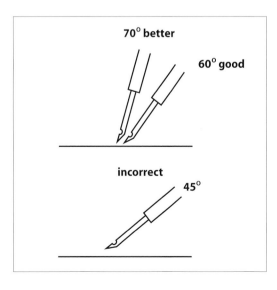

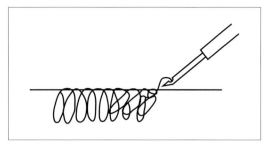

Working at a sharp angle tangles new loops with existing ones.

Pay attention to the front and back of the needle. The front of the needle is the angled or beveled edge and the back of the needle is the eye. Some needle handles are marked for easy identification (if yours isn't, a small dot of bright nail polish on the handle can accomplish the same thing). The thread comes out the back at the eye and leaves a path showing where the needle has been. Always face the angled edge (the front) into the next stitch. The direction of stitching doesn't matter as long as the front of the needle faces the new stitch. I will often move both my needle and hoop to get a more comfortable stitching position.

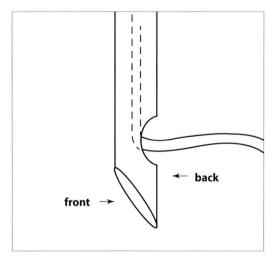

The front of the needle faces the new stitch; the back faces the completed stitch.

Your individual stitches and your rows of stitches need to be close enough together to cover the fabric on the right side. Some of the fabric will be visible between rows on the back. If you force too many stitches into an area, it will never lie flat.

When starting out, err on the side of too few stitches: It is better to have to add extra stitches later than to have too many to start with. As you continue doing punchneedle embroidery, you'll quickly develop an eye for the right density.

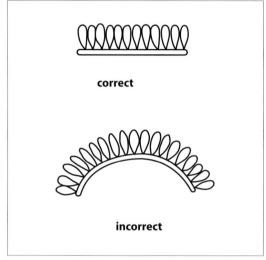

Crowding in too many stitches causes the fabric to roll instead of lying flat.

There is no knotting in punchneedle embroidery. When you finish an area or color, cut the thread even with the background fabric to stop. When you're first starting out, it's hard to believe the loops won't fall out. However, the friction between the loop threads and the base fabric keeps the loops in place without knotting or glue. You *can* pull the loops out if you aren't careful, but the embroidery is surprisingly durable—as the many vintage pieces of punchneedle embroidery testify. I have pieces of my own which look as good as new after 30 years. Just take reasonable care of them.

HOW DO THE STITCHES STAY IN THE FABRIC?

If you pull on the thread at the end of a row of punchneedle stitches, you can pull the loops out. This is a great feature when you've made a mistake and want to try again. But what keeps the stitches in place when you want them to stay?

The fabric you use is a key factor. It should be a tight, even weave, and should be stretched tautly in an embroidery hoop—but not so tightly the fabric is stretched out of shape or damaged. When you make a stitch, the needle pushes aside the weave and forces a loop into the space. When the needle is withdrawn, the natural elasticity in the fabric returns the weave to its original place, holding the loop in place.

Your stitching technique is another important factor. As you are stitching, keep the tip of the needle on the back of the fabric between stitches. Lifting the tip of the needle off the surface can pull out a loop or create a loop with a different height from the surrounding loops.

The embroidery on this shirt was done 30 years ago—and it is still neat and beautiful today!

Glue

To glue or not to glue; that is the question! Actually, it usually shouldn't be a question. If you are working with quality tools and the fabric hasn't been damaged, glue is unneeded and can even create problems—for instance, glue may make a piece of clothing with punchneedle embroidery unwashable.

If a needle manufacturer recommends finishing the embroidery with a coat of glue, I get suspicious. This usually means the needle tip is too sharp and may damage the fabric as you embroider. If the instructions that came with your needle recommend gluing the finished embroidery, I'd suggest looking for a different needle. None of the brands of needles I use ever mention glue as a necessity in their directions.

There is an exception to my rule of not gluing: the process for creating three-dimensional punchneedle pieces. Glue is a necessary element in this process; in fact, two different glue products (Fray-Check Seam Sealant and Gem-Tac embellishing glue) are used. It's impossible to secure the loops and create an edge which will not fray or ravel without some glue. The complete process will be described in chapter 4.

Blending and Clipping

Blending and clipping are two special stitching techniques used in some of the projects in this book.

Blending is using two or three different colored threads at once. Of course, this requires a needle which will hold more than one strand of floss or thread (i.e., #3 or #2/3 needle). This technique is used to create unique colors or to soften transitions between colors. The trout cigar box in the Gallery (see page 97) is an example of using many blended threads. Some of the three-dimensional flowers in the projects use this technique, too.

The other special technique used in this book is clipping or sculpting longer loops. Loops can be lengthened by resetting the gauge or stopper on the needle shaft (refer to the manufacturer's directions for specific instructions for how to do this with your needle). The more of the needle shaft that is exposed between the eye and the gauge or stopper, the longer the loops will be. You can use long loops in a design to create a contrast in texture, or you can cut their tops off to make a velvet–like texture. This is called clipping. Clipping will be used in some of the flowers and background elements in this book (for example, the embroidered necklace on page 32).

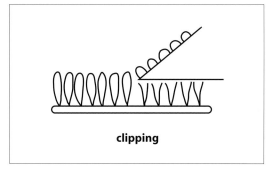

clipping

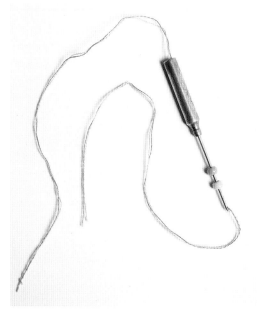

Two colors of thread in the needle.

Clipped loops. Notice how the color intensifies and darkens.

Sculpting is a variation of clipping that allows you to shape the velvety embroidery. Just trim the sides of an area shorter than the center, creating a domed or rounded area. Sculpting is used in several projects, including the bodies of the butterflies (see page 46). Specific instructions for these effects are included in the projects where they are used.

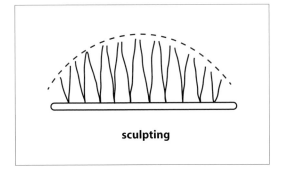

sculpting

Sculpted loops.

Caring for Punchneedle Embroidery

Treat punchneedle embroidery as you would any handwork—with respect. Keep it away from ring prongs, animal claws, and sharp or jagged edges. If an item needs pressing, place it facedown on a terry cloth towel. Press gently from the back. Steam may be used if needed. Gently fluff the loops with your fingertips. This process also works to remove or reduce ring marks made by stretching the embroidery in an embroidery hoop. Repeat the process as needed. This embroidery is surprisingly resilient.

As long as the background fabric is washable, the embroidered piece is washable. Washing actually helps the punchneedle loops stay in the fabric; it helps the weave tighten around the bases of the loops and gently felts the tiny hairs on each loop together with their neighbors. Punchneedle pieces may be hand washed or washed in a machine on the gentle cycle. Use a laundry bag or turn the piece inside out to protect the embroidery while in the machine. I don't usually wash silk, wool, or velvet, but I've never lost a loop because of not washing a piece. After a while you'll learn to trust the process and stop worrying about it.

CHAPTER 4
Three-Dimensional Punchneedle

This technique grew out of an "I wonder if I could . . . " moment. Was it possible, I wondered, to make three-dimensional punchneedle embroidery pieces? I wanted them to be completely freestanding and separate from any background. I started experimenting and found to my surprise that I could! Now that I know how to make it work, I can't stop thinking of new items to try.

Fantasy flower lapel pin.

Nature has always inspired me, so my first experiment was a stemmed flower. I wanted it to be tiny and delicate, and to have separate petals and leaves. The flower I designed is the one used in the beaded necklace (see page 43) and again on the napkin rings (see page 73). I'm still exploring flowers, as you'll see in a number of the projects. I like to see how close I can get to the real ones, but that doesn't mean everything has to be realistic. If you want to change colors but aren't sure what will

work, try this: Make a photocopy of the pattern and audition the colors using markers or colored pencils. It's much easier to make adjustments and changes *before* you start stitching.

The biggest hurdle in developing this method was figuring out how to keep the loops in the fabric once all the background fabric is cut away. When I cut away the background, the loops on the edges no longer had anything to keep them in place.

Glue solved that problem, but another unexpected problem showed up: A tiny edge of the fabric supporting the loops was visible once a piece was cut out. A light fabric edge under a piece of dark embroidery was very distracting. I realized that I needed to match the base fabric color to the embroidery. This minimized or eliminated the distracting contrast edge.

Light edge of fabric showing.

I also set up multiple pieces at the same time in one hoop. It's faster to make several of the same item at once instead of one at a time. Now I make all my flowers and leaves this way, stockpiling extras for future use.

The Basics of Making Three-Dimensional Pieces

Here is the basic process for making a three-dimensional embroidered piece.

1. The first step is to select a solid colored background fabric that matches the colors of your project. Any good-quality, solid-color cotton will work. It needs to be the same color on both sides—woven or dyed, not printed on one side. It also needs to be lightweight and tightly woven.

2. Next, trace the pattern pieces onto the fabric. Leave a scant ¼-inch margin around each piece. I use a fine lead pencil on light fabric and a silver or white fabric pencil on darks. If I'm making a number of pieces, I will make plastic templates of the pattern pieces to speed up the process. I label each piece and keep them in a resealable bag or envelope with the name of the item they belong to clearly visible. They can be reused indefinitely.

Multiples on fabric.

TIP » Put a piece of very fine sandpaper (220 grit) behind the fabric when you trace your pattern pieces. It stops the fabric from shifting while you are tracing.

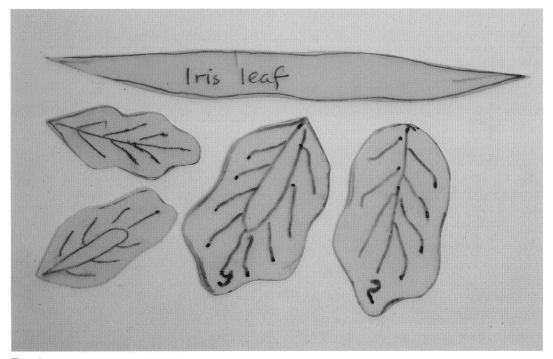

Templates.

3. Now it's time to embroider your design. Outline the edges of the pieces with a coordinating darker thread. I also use the same color for any details in the design. Next, I fill in the design with the primary color as directed or desired.

   I prefer to use a #1 needle for most pieces. I use a #3 needle with two threads when I need to blend colors. A #3 needle also works up faster. The loops are a little fatter, but only slightly. If you don't know which size has been used, it's sometimes hard to tell the difference.

4. When the embroidery is done, while it's still in the hoop, outline all of the edges of each pattern piece with a seam sealant. Let it dry, then apply a second coat—this is a "better safe than sorry" philosophy. I use Fray-Check for this step. It penetrates the fabric thoroughly and dries clear, without discoloring the stitches or fabric.

5. Once the edges are sealed and dry, the next step is to secure the loops in the fabric with glue. Use a flat, broad paintbrush to spread a thin layer of embellishing glue. I use Gem-Tac embellishing glue, which dries clear, remains flexible, and is waterproof and permanent. It shrinks slightly as it dries, locking the loops in the fabric. Also, there is no bleed-through to the front of the embroidery. Brush the glue beyond the edge of each piece into the margins of fabric to make sure everything is secure. Set aside to dry.

6. Once the glue is dry, the pieces are ready to be cut out. I use small, sharp, straight-blade embroidery scissors. Carefully cut out each piece as close as possible to the outline loops. Ideally, none of the background fabric will be visible on the edge.

7. To allow the pieces to be shaped, add floral wire to the back of each petal, leaf, or wing. Covered floral wire comes in green or white and in many weights and sizes. I use 28- and 32-gauge wire for this part of the process. I match the color of the wire to the piece: Green wire goes with everything green, and I hand color the white wire to match everything else (see page 10). First I precut my wire into the lengths I need, then I color it; once it's dry, I shape it to fit the piece and glue it in place on the back of the embroidered piece with more Gem-Tac. To ensure the pieces and the wire dry flat, I spread them out on a piece of aluminum foil, loop side down, add a second piece of foil on top, and weight them down with a large, heavy book or two. Once the pieces are dry and flat, they are ready to be assembled.

Back of a leaf with the floral-wire stem glued in place.

These three leaves show (from left to right) the 3-D punchneedle finishing process: edges sealed once, edges sealed a second time, and loops secured with a layer of glue.

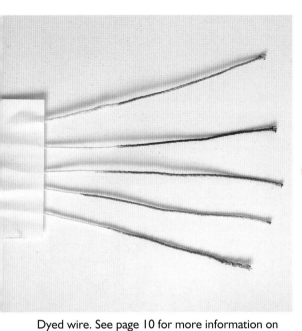

Dyed wire. See page 10 for more information on coloring wire to match your project.

BUTTERFLY WINGS

For the butterflies, the wire is shaped into one continuous length outlining both wings. It is bent to fit the contours of each wing. Once dry, the butterfly wings are shaped.

Back of a butterfly.

Pieces drying on foil.

8. Flowers need centers, or stamens. These are available in a variety of types and colors at craft stores. Arrange the petals around the stamens and secure them at the base with green floral tape. Then add a piece of 18- or 20-gauge green floral wire cut for a stem. Wrap the stem with floral tape, adding leaves as you go.

The piece is finished and ready to be displayed as-is or used in a larger project. The projects in this book include directions for lapel pins, small arrangements, headbands, napkin rings, and a decorated jewelry box. You may find inspiration for other creative projects of your own in the gallery at the end of the book. Let your imagination soar!

Petals secured around a stamen with floral tape.

PROJECT I

Batik Earrings

The easiest way to do punchneedle is to choose fabric with a good design and good color and reembroider it. Choosing thread colors isn't scary if you're just matching them to the fabric! Make sure the print of the fabric you choose is visible on the wrong side, because it will serve as the pattern. Pick a pretty section of the print and go to work!

The colors in this batik fabric caught my eye. A simple covered button form is used as the base. It can't get any easier!

Materials

Batik fabric
Embroidery floss: 1 skein Presencia #2406 or
    color to match fabric
#3 punchneedle
Covered button kit—1⅛" (2.8 cm) size
Pair of earring backs (clip or pierced)
All-purpose adhesive
Wire cutters or pliers

*See chapter 2 for more information on fabric, glue,
colored wire, and other materials.*

TIP » If you like the colors in this project but can't find the exact fabric I used, try a plain green background and work random areas in pink.

Pattern

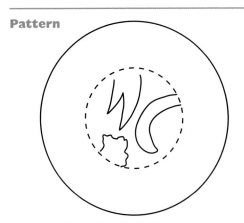

embroider inside dotted line for each earring

Directions

1. Cut out the half-circle pattern from the button kit.
2. Using the pattern, trace two full circles on the wrong side of the selected area of the fabric. Leave some space between them for cutting out the pieces. Put the fabric in your embroidery hoop.
3. Separate out three strands of floss from the skein and thread the needle with them. Fill in the desired areas on the fabric with punchneedle embroidery. Work to within ½" of the edge of the circle on all sides.
4. Cut out the circles on the traced lines.
5. From the excess fabric, cut out two more circles.

6. To assemble each earring, place the embroidered circle right side down. Place a plain fabric circle on top (this will add bulk for a good grip). Working with the two pieces as one, place the fabric right side down on the button mold, centered over the mold. Follow the button kit's directions for covering the form. Repeat for the second button.
7. Once the forms are covered, remove the metal shank from the back of each button using pliers or wire cutters. Glue on an earring back in its place. Let dry.

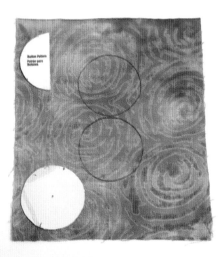

VARIATIONS

- Make a special set of buttons for a decorative addition to a jacket or vest. How pretty would that be?
- Covered buttons can also be used for pins or brooches. Cluster a few together with some metal buttons on a backing. Add a pin back and voilá, a one-of-a-kind original!

PROJECT 2
Pink Clover Earrings

Here's another pair of easy button earrings. I've added a flat-back jewel to these for sparkle, as well as some cut-out punchneedle leaves for extra dimension. If you can't find a fabric with a suitable print, no problem—I've also provided a pattern for the clover shape. The earrings can be easily and economically made. They're a wonderful gift for a special girlfriend.

Patterns

pink clover

leaf

make (2) for
each earring

TIP ❯❯ To prevent harsh transitions between pieces of variegated thread, start each new thread with the end that was cut from the piece of the thread you just finished. The transition becomes seamless!

See chapter 2 for more information on fabric, glue, colored wire, and other materials.

Materials

Flower-print cotton fabric
Solid green cotton fabric
Embroidery floss: 1 skein each
   of Presencia #2397, #2402,
   #4485, and #9860
#3 punchneedle
Covered button kit—1⅛"
   (2.8 cm) size
Pair of earring backs
   (clip or pierced)
Flat-back oval jewels
Seam sealant
All-purpose glue
Embellishing glue
Small paintbrush
Wire cutters or pliers

Directions

1. Cut out the half-circle pattern from the button kit.
2. Using the pattern, trace two full circles in the center of the fabric, each one centered over a motif. If using the clover flower pattern, trace the pattern in the center of each circle. Place the fabric in an embroidery hoop.
3. Using two strands of embroidery floss, outline the clover and work the veins using #2397. Fill in with two strands of #2402. Leave the center open for the jewel. Cut out the circles.
4. From the excess fabric, cut two more circles.
5. To assemble each earring, place the embroidered circle right side down. Place a plain fabric circle on top. Working with the two pieces as one, place the fabric right side down on the button mold, centered over the mold. Follow the button kit's directions for covering the form. Repeat for the second button.
6. Remove the button shank using pliers or wire cutters. Attach earring backs with all-purpose glue.
7. Using the leaf pattern, trace four leaves on the green fabric. Using two strands of #4485, outline the leaves and veins. Fill in with two strands of #9860. Work rows of embroidery up one side of the vein and down the other for a seamless color transition.

8. Following the procedure outlined in chapter 4, seal the edges with seam sealant. Let dry. Repeat.
9. Coat the back of each leaf with a light coat of embellishing glue. When everything is completely dry, cut out the leaves as close as possible to the embroidery.

10. Glue the jewel in the center of each clover with embellishing glue. Glue two overlapping leaves to the bottom edge of each earring with fabric glue.

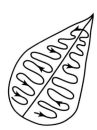

**stitching pattern
for variegated thread**

PROJECT 3

Reembroidered Necklace and Earrings

I fell in love with the lace-print fabric used in this piece—it's used for three different projects in the book. In this project, the flower motifs are completely embroidered and cut out. You'd never know a printed fabric was used for the designs. This black-and-white print is what I call a "coloring book" print. "Stay in-side the lines" and fill in the flowers with your favorite colors. I chose three different sizes of flowers to use—one large and two medium for the necklace, and two different small flowers for the ear-rings. I made a dozen of my own leaves to fill in the design.

The pieces of the necklace sit at different heights. The wired leaves are mounted on a card-board foundation piece. Small painted wooden pegs, concealed behind the flowers, lift the flowers above the leaves.

What's a necklace without beads? The hand-beaded fringe I added weights the front of the necklace, helping it hang cor-rectly and adding movement and shine. The fringe may be omitted if it's not your style. The embroi-dery hangs from a hand-beaded necklace (for a different look, you could substitute cording or ribbon in place of beads).

Materials

Fashion fabric (Michael Miller Fabrics
   pattern CX4595, "Zelda")
Solid green cotton fabric
Cotton fabric for covering the foundation
   (or use the same fabric as for the leaves)
Embroidery floss: 1 skein each of Presencia
   #5075, #9850, #1906, #1490, #1895,
   #1889, #1152, and #9100
#3 punchneedle
28-gauge green floral wire
Green felt
Cardboard (for foundation)
Quilt batting
Seven ³⁄₈" wooden furniture pegs
Green acrylic paint
3 mm green beads for the necklace (enough
   to string 18")
Crimping beads
Beading or polyester thread to match the beads
Assorted pearl, disc, faceted, and frosted red and
   pink beads (4 to 10 mm) for the fringe
21-strand beading wire, .014 diameter
Earring backs (clip-on or post)
Necklace clasp
Embellishing glue

All-purpose glue
Fabric glue
Silver or white fabric pencil
Small paintbrush
Beading needle
Needle-nose pliers
Wire cutters
Seam sealant

*See chapter 2 for more information on fabric, glue,
colored wire, and other materials.*

Directions

1. Select the flowers you want to use in the
   printed fabric or trace the flower patterns provided. Embroider the flowers using two strands
   of embroidery floss. Outline the flower petals
   and details with #1906. Fill in the petals from
   the center outward, starting with #1490, then
   using #1895, and changing to #1889 at the
   outer edge. Outline the centers with #1152.

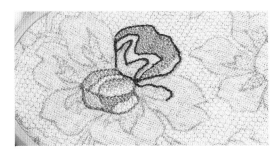

2. For the insides of the flower centers, reset the
   gauge or stopper on your needle (following the
   manufacturer's directions) to add ¼" to the distance between the needle's eye and the gauge
   or stopper. Work the centers with #9100. With
   sharp embroidery scissors, clip off the tops of
   the loops to create a velvet texture. Return the
   needle to its original setting.

Patterns

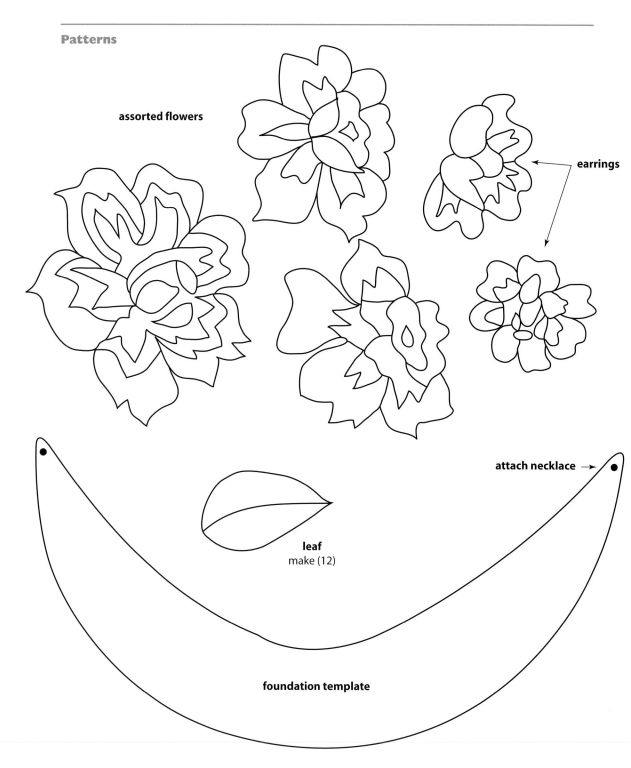

assorted flowers

earrings

leaf
make (12)

attach necklace →

foundation template

3. Trace 12 leaves (10 for the necklace and 2 for the earrings) onto the green cotton. Outline each leaf and vein with #5075. Fill in with #9850.

4. Seal the edges of all the flowers and leaves with seam sealant. Let dry. Repeat.

5. Coat the back of each piece with a thin layer of embellishing glue. Let dry.

6. Cut out each piece as close as possible to the embroidery. Set aside.

7. Cut twelve 1 to 1¼" pieces of floral wire. With embellishing glue, attach one piece to the back of each leaf. Let dry.

Assemble the Earrings

8. Use all-purpose adhesive to glue an earring back to each small flower. Cover the back with a small piece of green felt (if using a post back, push the post through the felt). Add one leaf to the bottom edge of each flower, as shown. Use the wire to shape the leaf to add dimension.

TIP ›› The actual fabric I used may be hard to find, so Michael Miller Fabrics LLC has kindly given me permission to reproduce some of the flowers to eliminate any frustration for you.

Assemble the Necklace

9. Trace the foundation template and cut out one from cardboard, one from batting, one from felt, and one from the background fabric. Add a ¼" seam allowance on all sides on the background fabric only.

10. Glue the batting to the cardboard using fabric glue. Lay out the background fabric, wrong side up. Place the cardboard and batting on the fabric, batting side down and centered on the fabric. Fold the seam allowance to the back and glue in place with fabric glue all around the edge. Clip the fabric along the curves to ease the fit, and trim the excess from the points to eliminate bulk. Cover the back of the cardboard with felt, trimming any excess felt even with the edge.

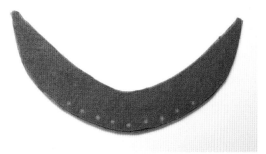

11. Thread a 12" length of beading wire through the end of the foundation piece. Thread a crimping bead onto one end of the wire and thread the other end of the wire back through the crimping bead. Crimp (smash) the bead with needle-nose pliers around both ends of wire to secure the wire in place as close as possible to the foundation piece. String beads on the wire to the desired length for half the necklace (mine is 9"). Add another crimping bead and one half of the necklace closure, then thread the wire back through the crimping bead and through several of the last few necklace beads. Pull snugly, then crimp the bead as close as possible to the necklace clasp. Trim off the excess beading wire. Repeat for the other side.

12. Paint the sides of the wooden pegs with green paint. Let dry.

13. Arrange the remaining ten leaves on the foundation as shown, five on each side (two at the tip and three on each side of the center flower). Glue the leaves in place at the bottom end of each leaf. Let dry.

14. Glue two pegs to the back of each of the medium flowers, and three pegs to the back of the large flower. Using embellishing glue, glue the large flower in the center space and the two medium flowers on each side. Shape the wired leaves to give the finished necklace a natural look.

15. Mark the center of the lower edge of the foundation, on the back of the piece, then mark four points on each side of the center, all $\frac{1}{2}$" apart. Add each strand of beaded fringe as follows. Thread a beading needle and anchor the thread on one of the spots you marked with a backstitch. String assorted fringe beads onto the thread until the fringe strand is the desired length. Run the thread around the last bead and back up through the other beads. Take another backstitch in the foundation where you started, then run the thread through the beads and back a second time. Take a third backstitch to anchor the thread and tie it off. Repeat for each individual strand of fringe, duplicating the bead placement in every strand (or every other strand) to create a pattern, or adding the beads randomly for a more casual look.

Beaded Heart Pin

Everyone loves hearts, and this punchneedle version with sparkly beads will be no exception. The addition of jump rings as well as a pin back lets you wear this piece as a pin or as a pendant. I like to embroider several hearts at once; they make wonderful handmade Valentine's Day gifts for friends. Pin the heart to a handmade card and surprise someone special!

TIP >> I recommend using polyester thread to sew the beads to this project; it provides more strength than cotton thread.

Materials

Mottled or batik fabric
Embroidery floss: 1 skein each of Presencia
    #9350, #2402, #2415, and #7471
#3 punchneedle
Assorted beads
Sewing thread to match beads
Cardboard
Quilt batting
Felt to match one of the colors in the fabric
Metal washer, 1" in diameter
Pin back, 1 to 1½" long
Two jump rings
Beading needle
Fabric glue
All-purpose adhesive

See chapter 2 for more information on fabric, glue, colored wire, and other materials.

Pattern

Directions

1. Trace the heart pattern onto the cardboard, and cut out. Use the cardboard heart as the template to trace the heart onto the back of the fabric. Set the cardboard heart aside.

2. Using two or three strands of embroidery floss in the #3 punchneedle, randomly embroider different areas in the heart, changing color as desired. Let some of the background fabric show for contrast and for space to add beads.

3. Using the beading needle, sew beads to different areas of the heart. Refer to the photo for ideas.

4. Cut out the heart, adding ¼" seam allowance around the edge.

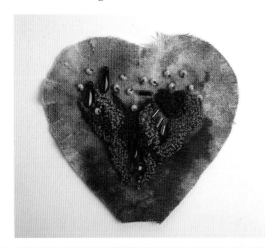

5. Using the cardboard heart from step 1 as a pattern, trace and cut out one heart from felt and two from quilt batting. Trim one batting heart ¼" smaller on all sides. Using fabric glue, glue the metal washer to the center of the cardboard heart, then glue the small batting heart on top of the washer, then glue the large batting heart over the small one.

6. Clip the seam allowance around the curves and in the dip in the top of the embroidered heart. Place the embroidered heart right side up and centered on the padded cardboard. Glue the clipped edges to the back with fabric glue. Trim the excess fabric from the tip to eliminate bulk, and fold the fabric at the tip over for a clean finish.

7. Glue the felt heart on the back of the piece using fabric glue. Trim away any excess felt even with the front.

8. Glue the pin back to the felt with all-purpose adhesive. Cut another small piece of felt to glue over the base of the pin back with fabric glue for a clean finish.

9. Join the two jump rings together so they interlock. Sew one ring to the felt backing just below the dip at the top of the heart to use it as a pendant. Sew seed beads end to end around the edge of the heart for extra texture.

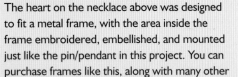

VARIATION

The heart on the necklace above was designed to fit a metal frame, with the area inside the frame embroidered, embellished, and mounted just like the pin/pendant in this project. You can purchase frames like this, along with many other jewelry findings, in craft stores and online.

PROJECT 5

Miniature Tiger Lily Lapel Pin

I've always loved tiger lilies. There is something about the spotted petals and the bright accent of orange in a garden that is hard to resist. In addition to these little flowers, you'll find another, larger tiger lily project later in the book (see page 54).

These miniature tiger lilies can be put to a variety of uses. You could put one in a tiny vase pin, as shown in this project, and wear it on a lapel, scarf, or hat. Make a few flowers with longer stems and display them in a tiny vase to brighten up a corner or bookshelf. Tie one on a package as an extra gift. Mount them on napkin rings or on a barrette. These are just a few ideas!

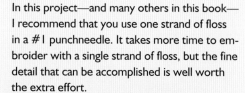

VARIATION

In this project—and many others in this book— I recommend that you use one strand of floss in a #1 punchneedle. It takes more time to embroider with a single strand of floss, but the fine detail that can be accomplished is well worth the extra effort.

However, if you want the embroidery to go more quickly or you want a less detailed look, you can always work the same projects using two strands of embroidery floss in a #3 punchneedle.

Materials

Solid cotton fabric in orange and green
Embroidery floss: 1 skein each of Presencia #1490, #7471, #1314, #1237, #7825, #4485, and #5400
#1 punchneedle
28-gauge green floral wire
32-gauge white wire, colored orange to match petals
20-gauge green floral wire
Green floral tape
Premade stamens
Metal bolo tie tip
Pin back, 1 to 1½" long
All-purpose glue
Seam sealant
Embellishing glue
Small paintbrush

See chapter 2 for more information on fabric, glue, colored wire, and other materials.

Patterns

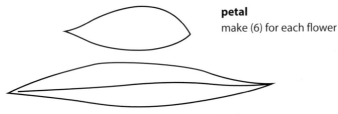

petal
make (6) for each flower

leaf
add 1–2 to each flower stem

VARIATION

If you can't find bolo tie tips, you can attach a pin back directly to the stem. Open the pin and wrap the stem and pin back together with floral tape to secure it in place. The pin back will be concealed behind the stem.

Directions

1. Trace six petals onto the orange cotton fabric. Trace one or two leaves onto the green cotton fabric.
2. Using one strand of floss in a #1 needle, outline each petal with #1490. Work three rows of #7471 on the outer edges of each petal. Fill in the center with #1237.

3. For the spots on the petals, reset the gauge on the needle to add ⅛" to the distance between the needle's eye and the gauge or stopper. Work spots with a single loop of #7825 randomly throughout each petal. Return the needle to its original setting.

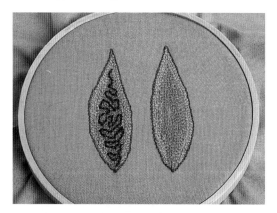

4. Outline the leaves with #4485, then fill them in with #5400.
5. Seal the edges of each piece with seam sealant. Let dry. Repeat.
6. Cover the back of each piece with a light coat of embellishing glue. Let dry.
7. Cut out the pieces as close as possible to the embroidery. Using embellishing glue, attach a 3½" length of 32-gauge orange-colored wire to the back of each petal. Attach a 5 to 6" length of 28-gauge green wire to the back of each leaf. Let dry.

8. Place the six petals evenly around the stamen. Wrap the bases of the petals with floral tape to secure. Attach the lily to a 4 to 5" stem of 20-gauge green wire.

9. Add the leaves to the lily stem using floral tape.
10. Glue the pin to the back of the bolo tie tip using all-purpose adhesive. Place the finished flower inside. The flower may be glued in place if desired.

Beaded Necklace with Three-Dimensional Flower

Among the craft supplies I collect are beads. When I get an idea for a piece, I go through my stash before going to the store. Believe it or not, everything used in this necklace came from my studio supplies. If I don't have to purchase anything new for a project, it feels like it's free.

It'd be impossible to duplicate this piece exactly, so it's provided as inspiration. Gather together some pretty beads and baubles and design your own one-of-a-kind necklace.

VARIATION

If you have trouble finding a suitable pendant vase, you could use a bolo tie tip with holes drilled through each side to string beading wire through. Or mount the flower on a pin back and pin it over a double strand of beads.

An alternate use of a single flower is this lapel pin.

Materials

Solid cotton fabric in fuchsia and green
Embroidery floss: 1 skein each of Presencia #5075, #9865, #2419, #2397, #2402, and #2415
#1 punchneedle
Black pearl premade stamen
28-gauge green floral wire
32-gauge white floral wire, colored magenta
Green floral tape
Small pendant vase
Assorted beads (enough to string two 14½" lengths)
Crimping beads
21-strand beading wire, .014 diameter
Necklace closure
Seam sealant
Embellishing glue
Small paintbrush
Needle-nose pliers
Wire cutters

See chapter 2 for more information on fabric, glue, colored wire, and other materials.

Directions

1. Trace five petals onto the fuchsia fabric. Trace four leaves onto the green fabric.
2. Using one strand of embroidery floss in the #1 needle, outline all the petals with #2419. Work two petals from light to dark—#2397, then #2402, then #2415—and work the other three petals in reverse order, from dark to light. Keep the transitions between the colors irregular for a lifelike look. Outline the leaves with #5075, and fill them in with #9865.

Patterns

petal
make (5) for each flower

leaf
make 3–4 for each stem

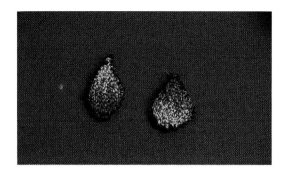

3. Seal all the edges of the petals and leaves with seam sealant. Let dry. Repeat.

4. Lightly coat the back of each petal and leaf with embellishing glue. Let dry.

5. Cut out all the pieces as close as possible to the embroidery. With embellishing glue, glue a 3 to 4" length of 28-gauge green wire to the back of each leaf and glue a 3" length of 32-gauge magenta wire to the back of each petal.

6. Evenly space the petals around the stamen and secure them at the bases with floral tape. Combine the leaves into one stem, with the leaves at different levels, using floral tape, then join the leaf stem to the flower stem. Trim the stem to fit your container. Glue in place.

7. Cut two 18" lengths of beading wire. Thread a wire through a crimping bead, then through the hole on one side of the pendant, and then back through the crimping bead. Crimp the bead on the wire to secure it, as close to the pendant as possible. String about 14½" of beads along the wire in whatever pattern or random order you prefer. Thread the wire through another crimping bead, then one half of the necklace closure, then through the crimping bead again. Crimp the bead as close as possible to the closure. Thread the extra beading wire back down through several beads, then cut off the tail. Repeat this process for the other side of the necklace.

8. Cut a 40" length of beading wire for the longer necklace strand. Attach one end to one side of the necklace closure with a crimping bead, as in step #7. String 35" of beads on the wire and fasten the end to the other half of the closure.

Monarch Butterfly Pin

Butterflies are like tiny flying paintings. In the past, I've been lucky enough to live in an area where monarch butterflies spent the winter. It is stunningly beautiful to see an entire grove of trees covered with over 100,000 of them. The air is filled with hundreds of them fluttering around in silence. It is spectacular!

Monarch butterflies have always been one of my favorites so of course I wanted to make some embroidered ones! These are slightly larger than life-size, but other than that, they are pretty accurate. This butterfly was made into a pin.

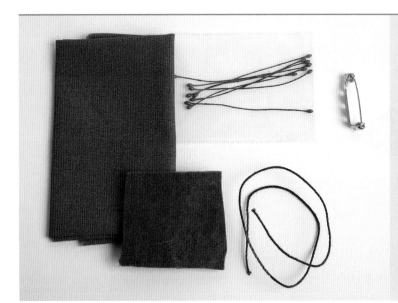

Materials

Solid orange cotton fabric
Embroidery floss: 1 skein each of Presencia #8756, #8032, #1000, and #7567
#1 or #3 punchneedle
Brown felt
32-gauge wire, colored orange
Double-ended stamen
Pin back, 1 to 1½" long
Seam sealant
Embellishing glue
Small paintbrush

See chapter 2 for more information on fabric, glue, colored wire, and other materials.

Pattern

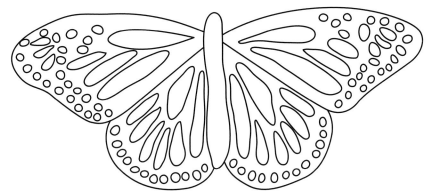

Directions

1. Transfer the butterfly pattern to the orange fabric. I used a light box, but an iron-on transfer or another of the methods described in chapter 3 would also work.

2. Using one strand of embroidery floss in a #1 needle, outline the wings and veins with #8756, then fill in the edges of the wings with the same color. Work all of the spots with #1000. Fill in the wings with #7567.

3. For the body, reset the gauge or stopper on the needle to add ¼" to the distance between the needle's eye and the gauge or stopper. Work the body densely with #8032. With sharp embroidery scissors, clip off the tops of the loops on the body to create a velvet texture.

4. Seal the edges of the wings with seam sealant. Let dry. Repeat

5. Lightly coat the back of the butterfly with embellishing glue. Let dry.

6. Cut out the butterfly as close as possible to the embroidery. With scissors, sculpt the body by trimming the sides of the body shorter, gradually leaving the threads longer toward the center of the body. This gives the body a rounded shape.

7. Shape a 7½ to 8" length of 32-gauge orange wire to the shape of the butterfly. Glue in place with embellishing glue. Let dry. Glue a folded double-ended stamen to the butterfly's head for antennae.

8. Glue a pin back to the back of the body. Cover the base of the pin back with a small piece of brown felt. Shape the wings as desired.

PROJECT 8
Fantasy Butterfly

I've given you my original color choices in the list of materials, but don't be afraid to play around with your own ideas. Turn this butterfly into your own one-of-a-kind piece!

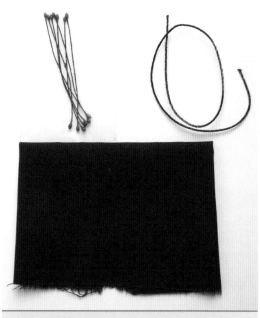

Larger than life and brightly colored, this butterfly is pure fantasy. It was one of my earliest three-dimensional punchneedle pieces. I haven't finished my butterfly into anything yet—I'm still deciding. Do I want another pin? Should I make it the centerpiece of a statement necklace? It might decorate a wall quilt or perch on a hat, handbag, or pillow. There are lots of possibilities!

This is a great project for playing with design and color. The colors I used in my butterfly, purple and yellow, are complementary—opposites on the color wheel. Try this project with your own choice of complementary colors, or experiment with other color schemes for different looks. An analogous color scheme (colors found next to each other on the color wheel), such as shades of blue and green, would be a little less dramatic. A monochromatic color palette (shades of one color) of tans and beiges with metallic gold or copper accents would look very sophisticated. Or you could go wild and embroider the butterfly entirely in metallic threads—how gorgeous would that be?

Materials

Solid purple cotton fabric
Embroidery floss: 1 skein each of Presencia
   #3327, #8083, #3068, #2615, #2705,
   #3822, #9100, #1109, #1068, and #7475
#3 punchneedle
32-gauge white wire, colored purple
Double-ended stamen
Finishing findings of your choice (pin back,
   beads for a necklace, etc.)
Seam sealant
Embellishing glue
Small paintbrush

See chapter 2 for more information on fabric, glue, colored wire, and other materials.

Pattern

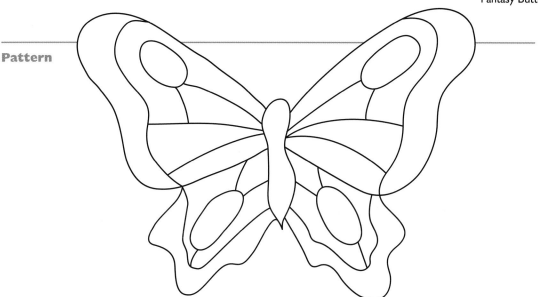

Directions

1. Transfer the design to the back of the fabric (see chapter 3 for possible methods; dressmaker's carbon paper or an iron-on transfer would be recommended).

2. Working with two strands of floss throughout, outline the wings and interior wing sections using #8083, then fill in the darkest area on the top wings with the same color. Use #3068 for the outer border of the top wings. Use #2705 for the bottom section of the top wings, and work the four spots with #3822. Use #2615 around the spots. Fill in the inner wing section on the top and bottom wings with #9100. The outer edge of the bottom wing is worked in #1109. The top section of the bottom wing is #1068 and the bottom section is #7475.

3. For the body, reset the gauge or stopper on the needle to add ¼" to the distance between the needle's eye and the gauge or stopper. Work the body densely with #8083. With sharp embroidery scissors, clip off the tops of the loops to create a velvet texture.

4. Seal the edges of the wings with seam sealant. Let dry. Repeat.

5. Cover the back of the butterfly with a light coat of embellishing glue. Let dry.

6. Cut out the butterfly as close as possible to the embroidery. With scissors, sculpt the body by trimming the sides of the body shorter, gradually leaving the threads longer toward the center of the body. This gives the body a rounded shape.

7. Bend a 13" length of 32-gauge purple-colored wire to match the shape of the butterfly. Glue in place with embellishing glue. Glue a double-ended stamen folded in half to the top of the body for antennae.

8. Finish the butterfly as a pin or necklace, or display it as is.

Eastern Tailed Blue Butterfly Pins

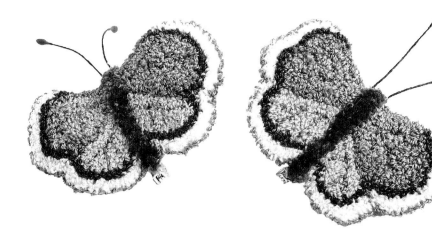

The eastern tailed blue butterfly is tiny: Its wingspan is about an inch. These butterflies are very abundant on the East Coast of the United States—but we even have them in Texas. They frequent gardens and puddles of water. How can anyone resist a tiny blue butterfly?

This version is almost twice the size of the real-life butterfly, with a wingspan of 1¾"—still pretty small. Two of these casually pinned to a jacket or sleeve would be delightful. I may pin my pair to the bluebell quilt block pillow (see page 76) to add a touch of whimsy and dimension. I can always remove them to wear, but I get to enjoy them in the meantime on the pillow.

Pattern

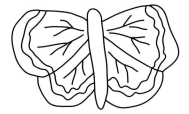

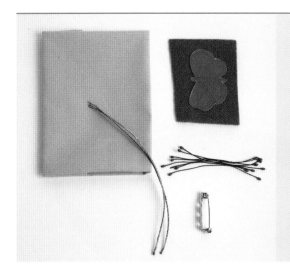

Materials

Solid gray or white cotton fabric
Embroidery floss: 1 skein each Presencia #3387,
 #3396, #3400, #1000, #8785, and #8705
#1 or #3 punchneedle
Gray felt
32-gauge wire, colored blue
2 double-ended stamens
2 pin backs, 1" long
Seam sealant
Embellishing glue
Small paintbrush

*See chapter 2 for more information on fabric, glue, colored
wire, and other materials.*

Directions

1. Transfer the butterfly pattern twice to the background fabric. I traced it using a light box, but you could use any of the methods in chapter 3.
2. Outline each butterfly and embroider the veins in the wings with #8785. Embroider the outer rim of each wing with #1000, then work two rows of #8705 along the edges of the wings. Work the lower wings with #3387. Outline all the veins of the upper wings with #3396. Fill in the remaining areas of the wings with #3400.
3. For the butterfly bodies, reset the gauge or stopper on the needle to add ¼" to the distance between the needle's eye and the gauge or stopper. Embroider the bodies densely with #8785.
4. With sharp embroidery scissors, clip off the tops of the loops to give the bodies a velvet texture.
5. Seal the edges of the wings with seam sealant. Let dry. Repeat.
6. Lightly coat the back of each butterfly with embellishing glue. Let dry.

7. Cut out the butterfly as close as possible to the embroidery. With scissors, sculpt the body area by trimming the sides of the body shorter, gradually leaving the threads longer toward the center of the body. This gives the bodies a rounded shape.
8. Shape a 3½" length of 32-gauge blue wire to the outline of the open wings. Glue in place with embellishing glue. Let dry.
9. Glue a pin back to each butterfly, along the back of the body. Cover the base of the pin back with a small piece of gray felt. Glue a double-ended stamen folded in half to the back of each head for antennae.

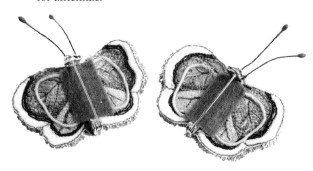

Camellia Headband

This headband has a classic appearance with a bit of snap. This peppermint camellia looks great against the black satin. If you add a small black veil and a few feathers, this accessory becomes a "fascinator." When worked in all white, it could be a bridal headpiece. If a headband doesn't appeal to you, this same flower looks pretty as a bloom in a vase or as a lapel pin.

See chapter 2 for more information on fabric, glue, colored wire, and other materials.

Materials

Solid white cotton fabric

Embroidery floss: 1 skein each of Presencia #1000, #9395, and #8400

#1 punchneedle

32-gauge white wire

Green floral tape

Pearl stamen

Purchased black satin headband

¾ yd. double-faced black satin ribbon, 1" wide

2 purchased satin leaves

Seam sealant

Embellishing glue

Small paintbrush

Fabric glue

Clothespin

Patterns

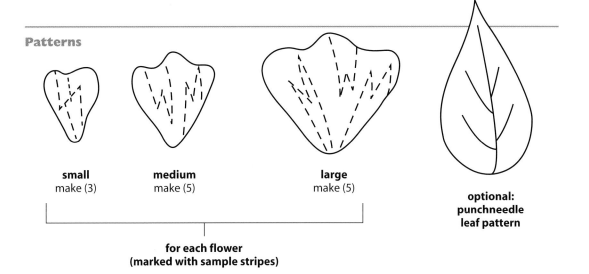

small
make (3)

medium
make (5)

large
make (5)

**optional:
punchneedle
leaf pattern**

**for each flower
(marked with sample stripes)**

Directions

1. Trace three small, five medium, and five large petals on white cotton.

2. Using one strand of embroidery floss in a #1 needle, outline each petal with #8400. Randomly work irregular areas on each petal using #9395 (use the photo as a reference). The variegated thread adds realism to this flower—no two petals will be alike. Fill in the rest of each petal with #1000.

3. Seal all the edges of the petals with seam sealant. Let dry. Repeat.

4. Lightly coat the backs of the petals with embellishing glue. Let dry.

5. Cut out each petal as close as possible to the embroidery. For each small petal, glue a 2½ to 3" length of 32-gauge white wire to the back with embellishing glue. For each medium petal, wrap a 4" length of wire around your fingertip to make a loop. For each large petal, shape a 5 to 6" length of wire into a loop that will fit just inside the outer edges of the petal. Glue one wire loop to each petal. Let dry.

6. Arrange the three small petals around the stamen and attach them at the base with floral tape. Evenly space the five medium petals around the center and secure with more floral tape. Finally, arrange the five large petals, evenly spaced, around the outside of the flower. Again, attach them with floral tape. Add two satin leaves in the same manner. Curl the finished stem around a pencil to give it the shape you want. Shape the petals.

7. Glue the flower to the headband with fabric glue. Hold in place with a clothespin until dry.

8. Wrap the satin ribbon around the headband and the flower stem and tie it in a bow. Cut a V in the ends to finish.

Tiger Lily Jewelry Box

The tiger lily featured in this project is larger than the one in project 5, and has more subtle shading (if the word "subtle" can be applied to a bright orange flower!). My goal was to make it look like the lily had just been picked and laid on top of a lovely jewelry box. As a play on "tiger" lily, I machine quilted tiger-striped fabric print for the window on top of the box. A few gold and silver charms allude to the jewelry inside. A life-size bumblebee appears to hover over the flower looking for nectar. The stargazer lily from the tote bag project (page 69) could easily be substituted for the tiger lily for a monochromatic look. Either flower would also look beautiful tucked into a fabulous hairdo.

Materials

Solid cotton fabric in orange and green

Tiger print cotton fabric for background
(optional)

Embroidery floss: 1 skein each of Presencia
#8083, #7580, #1314, #1325, #7567,
#4485, and #5400

#3 punchneedle

20-gauge green floral wire

28-gauge green floral wire

32-gauge white wire, colored orange

Green floral tape

Quilt batting

Leather jewelry box with window
(see Resources, page 103)

Metallic gold craft cord

3 metal heart charms

Purchased artificial bumblebee (optional)

Seam sealant

Embellishing glue

Small paintbrush

All-purpose glue

Premade flower stamen

*See chapter 2 for more information on fabric, glue,
colored wire, and other materials.*

Patterns

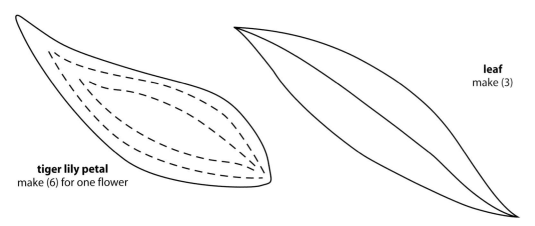

tiger lily petal
make (6) for one flower

leaf
make (3)

Directions

1. Cut a piece of tiger print fabric ½" larger on all sides than the window in the jewelry box. Cut a piece of quilt batting the same size. Place the fabric right side up on top of the batting. Hand or machine quilt the two layers together. Trim the quilted fabric to ¼" larger than the window on all sides.

2. Following the directions that came with the jewelry box, remove the protective paper from the window and insert the quilted fabric. Using embellishing glue, glue a length of gold craft cord around the opening, begining and ending in the lower right corner. Tuck the raw ends under the window opening. Using all-purpose adhesive, glue the charms in the lower right corner to conceal the ends of the cord. Set the box aside.

3. Trace six petals onto the orange cotton. Trace three leaves onto the green cotton.

4. Using two strands of embroidery floss in the #3 needle, outline each petal with #7580. Working from the outer edge of the petal inward, start filling in the petal with two or three rows of #1314, then work two rows using one strand of #1314 and one of #1325. Work the next two rows with two strands of #1325, then work the next two rows with one strand of #1325 and one of #7567. Fill in the center of the petal with #7567.

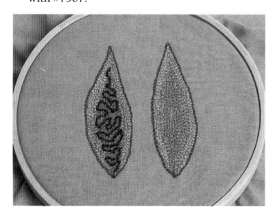

5. For the spots on the petals, reset the gauge or stopper on your punchneedle to add a generous ⅛ to 3⁄16". Thread the needle with two strands of #8083. Punch spots randomly on each petal. Return the gauge or stopper to its original setting.

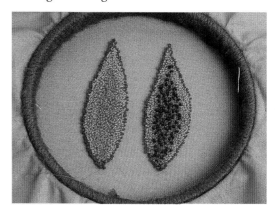

6. Outline each leaf with #4485. Fill in the leaves with #5400.

7. Seal the edges of each petal and leaf with seam sealant. Let dry. Repeat.

8. Cover the back of each piece with embellishing glue. Let dry.

9. Cut out the petals and leaves as close as possible to the embroidery. With embellishing glue, glue a 4½ to 5" length of 32-gauge orange wire to the center back of each petal. Glue a 5 to 5½" piece of 28-gauge green wire to the back of each leaf.

10. When all the glue is dry, arrange the six petals evenly around the stamen. Wrap them with floral tape to secure. Attach the lily to a 4 to 5" 20-gauge green wire stem with more floral tape, then attach the leaves to the stem. Curl the stem around a pencil to give it a nice shape.

11. Arrange the lily as desired on the top of the box. Glue in place using embellishing glue. If adding a bumblebee, glue the end of its wire under the craft cord and bend the wire so the bumblebee is in midair.

Hydrangea Needle Case

I came up with this project when I needed a place to keep my punchneedles between projects. I've had a needle box for years, but it was tiny, and my collection of needles had grown and evolved. My #6 needles didn't fit in it at all, and I had to keep a separate container for all of the threaders.

One day, I put away a new piece of jewelry and was about to throw out the hinged box it had come in when I realized I might be able to use it for my needles. Recycling (or upcycling) to the rescue! I tested it to see what would fit inside, and to my surprise there was room for everything and more. This little box (4 by 3¼ by 1½") holds six #6 needles, a package of assorted gauge sleeves, a tiny ruler, magnetic strips for the threaders, a small emery strawberry, embroidery scissors, *and* my original needle box containing nine more needles. It was perfect—it just needed to be pretty.

For this project, I drew a close-up of some hydrangea blossoms. I've worked mine in blue, but they also grow in pink, white, and chartreuse with misty burgundy edges. I sewed a seed bead in the center of each floweret and framed the embroidery with gold cord and four leaf beads. I've also included an alternate design for this box—for this one, you'll have to choose the colors.

My needle case is now easy to find and easy to take with me, and looks great on a table when I'm teaching or demonstrating.

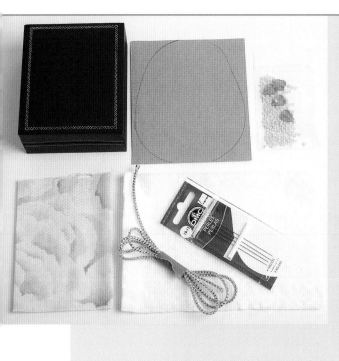

Materials

Cotton fabric for background

Embroidery floss: 1 skein each of Presencia #2720, #3068, #2705, #2732, #1094, #5075, and #9865

#1 punchneedle

Hinged box (4 by 3¼ by 1½")

Piece of cardboard cut to fit your box (mine is 1⅞ by 2⅝")

3 pieces of quilt batting, 1⅞ by 2⅝", 1½ by 2¼", and 1 by 1½" (adjust to fit your box as needed)

12" piece of gold cording (or cut to fit your box)

6 yellow seed beads

4 leaf beads

Sewing thread

Seam sealant

Embellishing glue

Fabric glue

Beading needle

See chapter 2 for more information on fabric, glue, colored wire, and other materials.

Patterns

Directions

1. Trace the design onto the wrong side of the fabric using the transfer method of your choice (see chapter 3).
2. Outline the flowers with one strand of #2705. Work all the veins in the petals with #3068. Fill in the base of each petal halfway, creating an irregular edge, with #2705. Complete the outer portion of each petal with #2732, intermingling some loops of #2732 with the loops of #2705 to blur the transition. Outline the leaves and veins with #5075. Fill in with #9865. For seamless transition between pieces of variegated thread, start each new thread with the same color as the end of the previous thread (light to light, dark to dark).

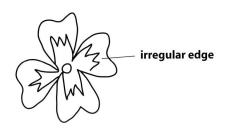

— **irregular edge**

3. For the centers of the flowers, reset the gauge or stopper on the needle to add $1/8$" to the distance between the needle's eye and the gauge or stopper. Stitch the centers with #1094. Using the beading needle, sew one yellow seed bead in the middle of the cluster of longer loops.
4. Glue smallest piece of batting to the center of the cardboard with fabric glue. Place the medium piece on top and glue in place, then glue on the largest piece.

5. Press the finished embroidery facedown on a terry cloth towel. Trim the embroidery to fit the cardboard, leaving a $1/2$" seam allowance on all sides. Center the embroidery right side up over the cardboard. Glue the seam allowance to the back using fabric glue. Trim and miter the corners to reduce bulk. Glue the embroidery-covered cardboard to the top of the box.
6. Trim the embroidered piece with the gold cord, gluing the cord down with fabric glue. Add leaf beads on each corner, if desired, with embellishing glue.

Morning Glory Journal

Materials

Blank journal

8 by 9" piece of background fabric—silk noil, Weaver's Cloth, tussah silk, solid cotton, or silk dupioni

Piece of iron-on white nylon tricot interfacing 4 by 6" (if using silk or dark fabric)

Embroidery floss: 1 skein each of Presencia #4485, #9860, #3411, #1000, #4799, #3387, #8400, #3400, #1109, and #8075

#3 punchneedle

Piece of cardboard 5 by 2½"

Piece of batting 5 by 2½"

2 black seed beads

1 yellow seed bead

Black and white sewing thread

½ yard piping (with or without a flange)

Embellishing glue

Fabric glue

Tracing paper

Iron-on transfer pencil

Iron

White or silver fabric pencil

Beading needle

See chapter 2 for more information on fabric, glue, colored wire, and other materials.

There used to be a fence not far from my house that was covered in a blanket of blue morning glories. The flowers appeared suddenly in early summer and took your breath away. There aren't many flowers with this deep, rich blue in nature, so their color adds to their mystique. One popular variety is aptly named "Heavenly Blue." That fence was my inspiration for this project.

Morning glory flowers don't last very long, especially in our Texas heat. They can't be used as cut flowers. Their beauty is very fleeting. The morning glory in this project, however, can be kept around and enjoyed indefinitely, whether it decorates a journal cover or some other item or is framed and hung on a wall.

Pattern

Directions

1. If you are using silk or other delicate fabric, or a dark-colored fabric, iron the nylon tricot interfacing to the back of the fabric following the manufacturer's directions. (You can skip this step if you're using light-colored cotton or Weaver's Cloth).

2. Following the manufacturer's directions, trace the pattern on tracing paper with the iron-on transfer pencil. Place the image facedown on the back of the tricot or fabric, and hold the

iron in place over it until the pattern transfers to the back of the tricot or fabric. Do not slide the iron back and forth over the pattern; this can cause the image to shift and the lines of the design to blur.

3. Using two strands throughout in a #3 needle, outline all the leaves and stems with #4485, then fill them in with #9860. (For a seamless color transition between pieces of variegated thread, start each new piece with the same color as the preceding piece ended with— light to light, dark to dark.)

4. Use #3411 for the dark details on the flower and bud. Work the base of the trumpet with #8400. Fill in the trumpet, the star on the face of the flower, and the bee's wings with #1000. Use #4799 for the center of the flower. Use #3387 for the inner portion of the flower's throat. Use one strand of #3387 and one of #3400 blended together to work the transition area. Stitch three to four rows with the blended threads, then finish the blossom with #3400. For the bud, add a row of #3400 on each side of the twist lines; fill in the remaining areas of the bud with #3387. Work alternating bands of #1109 and #8075 for the bee's body.

5. Draw tendrils freehand on the front of the embroidery with a white or silver fabric pencil. From the *front,* embroider the tendrils, punching the loops to the back. These flat (reverse) stitches look like backstitch and add a contrast in texture.

6. Working from the front and using the beading needle and black thread, sew one black seed bead to each side of the bee's head for eyes. Add two or three 1/8" long legs to each side of the bee. Change to white thread and sew one yellow seed bead to the center of the flower.

7. Cut out the embroidered piece, leaving a seam allowance of 1/2" on all sides. Glue the batting to one side of the cardboard with fabric glue. Place the embroidery right side down. Place the cardboard, batting side down, on top of it, with the design centered. Fold the fabric to the back and glue the edges in place with fabric glue. Trim the excess fabric from the corners, miter the corners, and glue in place.

8. If the cording has a flange, glue it to the back of the cardboard around the edge. Clip the flange to ease the cord around the corners. Overlap the ends and tuck them to the back. Glue the finished embroidery to the journal as shown.

   If the cording does not have a flange, glue the mounted embroidery right side up to the journal, then add the cording around the design with fabric glue. Tuck the cut edges of the cording behind the cardboard.

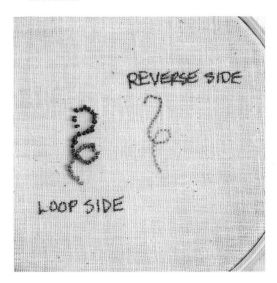

PROJECT 14
Photo Album

In this project, the design is provided by pre-printed fabric. I loved the elements in this simple damask print. The two-tone fabric matched the color of the cover of the album. There are lots of damask fabrics available. Use my project as an inspiration and choose a print that appeals to you.

Two-tone prints offer lots of color possibilities. I chose cheerful, bright colors for my album, but don't be afraid to add your own personality to this project. The two-color print used here would be elegant worked in tones of white with some metallic pearl thread worked into it. In tones of aqua, it would be soft and subtle. Adding black and coral to the aqua and white would give the album a more dramatic look. Each color combination creates a different mood and style.

Materials

Two-tone cotton print fabric
Embroidery floss: 1 skein each of Presencia #4485, #9865, #9060, #1915, #1895, #1307, #7580, and #1325
#3 punchneedle
Photo album with a window in the cover
Cardboard cut to fit window
Two pieces of quilt batting cut to same size as cardboard
Fabric glue

See chapter 2 for more information on fabric, glue, colored wire, and other materials.

Directions

1. Select an area of fabric to embroider. Mark an area on the fabric that fits in the window on the front of the album, then put the fabric in your hoop.

2. Embroider the design, using three strands of embroidery floss in a #3 needle. In my piece, I outlined the leaves with #4485 and filled them in with #9865. The pink petals were outlined with #1915 and filled in with #1895, and the orange petals were outlined with #7580 and filled in with #1325. The top petals were worked in #1307, with #7580 for the outline. I filled in the center area with #9060.

3. Following the manufacturer's directions, adjust the gauge or stopper on your needle to add $1/4$" to the distance between the needle's eye and the gauge or stopper. Work the stamens with #9060.

4. Once your design is complete, press right side down on a terry cloth towel.

5. Cut two pieces of quilt batting the same size as the piece of cardboard, then trim $1/2$" from each side on one piece. Glue the smaller piece to the center of the cardboard, then glue the larger piece on top.

6. Center the embroidery over the cardboard piece. Cut out the embroidered panel, leaving a seam allowance of $1/2$" on all sides. Place right side up on the padded side of the cardboard. Glue the seam allowance to the back of the cardboard with fabric glue, trimming and mitering the corners for a clean edge.

7. Inset the embroidered panel in the window of the album to finish. You can glue it in place if desired, or skip this step to leave the option of changing it out later.

PROJECT 15
Clam Shell Coin Purse

Having coordinating accessories for a handbag always looks polished. The fabric used here is the same print as the embroidered insert in the handbag on page 67. (It's also the basis for the necklace and earring set on page 32). Buy plenty of your favorite fabric and make a matching set of accessories!

The black lace motif in this fabric is pretty and feminine. I covered some of the flowers with punchneedle embroidery and left other areas of the lace background showing. The background and the punchneedle areas complement each other.

Clover Needlecraft makes a wonderful kit for a clam shell accessory case. It's available in three sizes; here I used the medium size (2½ by 4 by 2½"/65 by 100 by 65 mm). We will be focusing only on the embroidery here. The directions for making the coin purse itself come with the kit, along with the plastic pieces which are necessary to make the purse spring open. Look for a kit in your local needlework or fabric store or contact Clover Needlecraft (see Resources, page 103) for a source near you.

Materials

Fabric of choice (I used Michael Miller Fabrics CX4595, "Zelda")
Cotton fabric for lining
Embroidery floss: 1 skein each of Presencia #5075, #4565, #4561, #1906, #1490, #1895, #1889, #1152, and #9100
#3 punchneedle
Clam shell accessory case kit (see Resources, page 103)
Additional materials and supplies for constructing the clamshell purse will be given on the kit packaging.

See chapter 2 for more information on fabric, glue, colored wire, and other materials.

Directions

1. Following the manufacturer's directions, trace the template pieces from the kit onto the fabric for the outside of the purse.

2. Using two strands of the embroidery floss in a #3 punchneedle throughout, outline the leaves with #5075. Fill them in with two shades, using #4565 as the medium tone and #4561 as the light; refer to the photos below for placement of the colors. Outline the flowers with #1906. Fill in the petal areas using, from the center out, #1490, #1895, and #1889. Outline the center of the flowers with #1152.

3. For the stamen areas, reset the gauge or stopper, following the manufacturer's directions, to add ¼" to the distance between the needle's eye and the gauge or stopper. Work the stamen areas

with #9100. With sharp embroidery scissors, clip off the tops of the loops to create a velvet texture.

4. Refer to the kit for directions for assembling the clam shell purse.

Embroidered Inset Handbag

A black leather handbag is a staple of most every woman's wardrobe. This one's silhouette is classic and ladylike, but the unexpected beaded and embroidered panel on the front gives it a modern touch. The fabric is the same used in the Clam Shell Coin Purse (see page 65). For more versatility, you could make a few different insets and switch them out to match specific outfits.

Materials

Cotton print fabric (I used Michael Miller Fabrics CX4595, "Zelda")

Embroidery floss: 1 skein each of Presencia #5075, #4565, #4561, #1906, #1490, #1895, #1889, #1152, and #9100

#3 punchneedle

Black handbag with 3½ by 8" window (see Resources, page 103)

Piece of batting 4½ by 9"

24" length of fused pearls or cross-locked black beads

Faceted seed beads

Beading needle and black thread

Washable fabric marker

See chapter 2 for more information on fabric, glue, colored wire, and other materials.

Directions

1. Make a paper template of the window. Use the template to try out different areas of the fabric to embroider. Once you've selected an area, mark the window outline around it with a washable fabric marker. Be sure to leave enough room on the sides to allow you to put the fabric in an embroidery hoop.

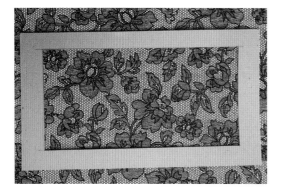

2. Using two strands of embroidery floss in a #3 needle, embroider the design. Outline the leaves with #5075 and fill them in using #4561 and #4565. Outline the flowers with #1906. Use #1490, #1895, and #1889 to fill in the petals, working from the center to the edge and from dark to light. Outline the outer flower centers with #1152 and fill these areas in with #9100.

3. For the stamen areas, reset the gauge or stopper to add ¼" to the distance between the needle's eye and the gauge or stopper. Work the stamen areas with #9100. With sharp embroidery scissors, clip off the tops of the loops to make a velvet texture.

4. Trim the fabric to 5 by 10" (or 1" larger on each side than the window on your handbag). Place the batting behind the embroidery, centered, and free motion–quilt or hand-quilt the piece. Trim the quilted piece to 4½ by 9" (or ½" larger on each side than the window).

5. With the beading needle, hand sew faceted seed beads at random on the background. Hand tack the fused pearls or cross-locked beads around the edge to fit just inside the opening.

6. Remove the protective covering on the handbag inset to reveal the adhesive. Insert the finished embroidery. Tuck the raw edges behind the edge of the window. Align the beads with the edges of the opening.

Stargazer Lily Tote Bag

I often need tote bags to carry my projects around—but I don't like them to look utilitarian. Even the very expensive ones are rarely beautiful. This doesn't need to be the case!

I liked the styling and shape of this canvas tote, as well as the fact that it had a window where I could put a piece of embroidery. When I considered what to put in that window, I didn't want something traditional or expected. A stargazer lily was perfect, with its dramatic coloring—white-edged petals gradually shading to dark magenta, each petal speckled with dark burgundy. The fragrance is heavenly, but I can't capture that. I juxtaposed the lily against a subtle dark animal print which I embellished with embroidery as well; some of the spots have had the loops clipped for a velvet texture.

Materials

Solid cotton fabric in green and white
Cotton print fabric—small-scale leopard/ cheetah print or other background fabric
Embroidery floss: 1 skein each of Presencia #8072, #8080, #5084, #9865, #1000, #2390, #2314, #2323, #2333, and #2171
#3 punchneedle
28-gauge green floral wire
32-gauge white floral wire, colored pink
Green floral tape
Purchased stamen
Canvas tote bag with 3½ by 8" window (see Resources, page 103)
Piece of quilt batting 4½ by 9"
Seam sealant
Embellishing glue
Small paintbrush
Fabric glue

See chapter 2 for more information on fabric, glue, colored wire, and other materials.

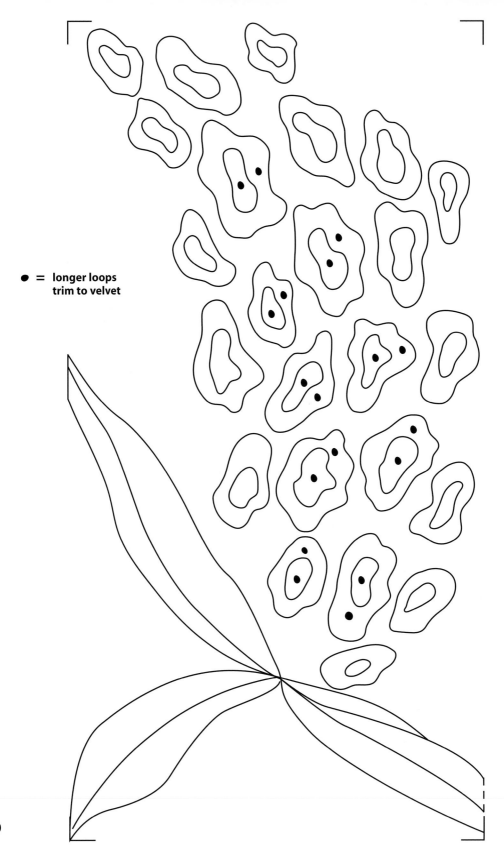

● = **longer loops
trim to velvet**

Patterns

Stargazer Lily Petal
make (6)

dots indicate transition areas

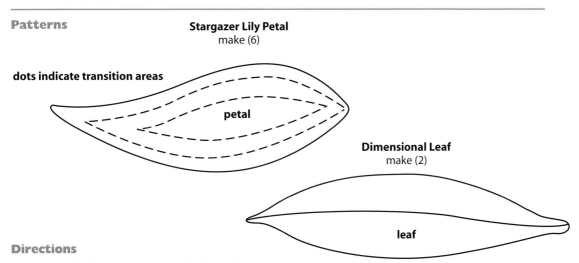

petal

Dimensional Leaf
make (2)

leaf

Directions

1. Transfer the leaves and spots to the back of the printed fabric using the method of your choice (see chapter 3).

2. Using two strands of embroidery floss through-out, work the outer rings of the spots with #8080 and fill in the centers with #8072. Work 16 assorted spots, leaving 7 larger spots in the middle (marked with dots on the pattern) unstitched.

3. Reset the gauge or stopper on the needle to add ¼" to the distance between the needle's eye and the gauge or stopper. Work the remaining spots in the same colors as the small spots, using the longer setting. With sharp embroidery scissors, clip off the tops of the long loops to create a velvet texture. Return the gauge or stopper to the regular setting.

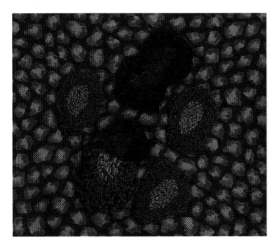

4. Work the veins and the outlines of the leaves with #5084 and fill them in with #9865.

5. Center the quilt batting on the wrong side of the background. Baste to hold in place. Free motion machine-quilt or hand-quilt the fabric to the batting. Trim the completed piece to 4½ by 9" (or to fit the opening).

6. Following the directions that came with the tote bag, remove the protective covering in the window to expose the adhesive. Insert the background fabric into the window. Tuck the excess behind the edges of the window. Set aside.

7. Trace two leaves onto the green cotton fabric. Embroider them in the same colors as the leaves on the background print.

8. Trace six petals onto the white cotton fabric. To create the subtle color transitions in the petals, two colors of thread will be blended for a few rows on every color change. For each petal, start in the center with two strands of #2333. Work several rows, then use one strand of #2333 and one of #2323 for two rows. Next, work two rows of two strands of #2323. For the next transition, use one strand of #2323 and one of #2314; again, work with the blended colors for two rows, then work two rows of all #2314. Next, work two rows of one strand of

#2314 and one of #2390 and then two rows of all #2390. For the last transition, use one strand of #2390 and one of #1000. Finish the outer edge of the petal with all #1000. Embroider the other five petals in the same way.

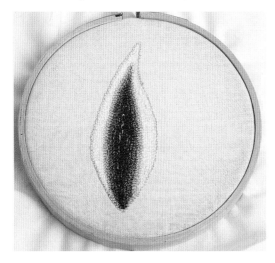

9. For the spots on the petals, reset the gauge or stopper on your needle to add 1/8" to the distance between the needle's eye and the gauge or stopper. With #2171, add spots at random on each petal. Carry the thread snugly along the back of the work between stitches; the stitches should be no more than 1/4" apart.

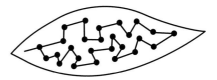

10. Seal all the edges of the petals and leaves with seam sealant. Let dry. Repeat.
11. Lightly coat the back of each piece with embellishing glue. Let dry.
12. Cut out all the pieces as close as possible to the embroidery.
13. Glue a piece of 28-gauge green floral wire to the back of each leaf, leaving a stem of about 1" of wire extending beyond the base of the leaf. Glue 32-gauge wire, colored to match the flower, to the back of each petal, again leaving a stem of about 1".
14. Arrange three petals evenly spaced around the stamen. Wrap with green floral tape to secure. Add the remaining three petals, offset between the first set of petals, and secure with floral tape. Attach the two leaves on one side, using floral tape.
15. Attach the flower to the background using fabric glue, leaving the petals and leaves free. Once the flower is secure, arrange the petals and leaves, attatching their tips to the background with more fabric glue. Let dry.

Flower Napkin Rings

Everything tastes better when you share a meal with friends or family at a beautifully set table. These decorative napkin rings, filled with pretty lace-edged napkins, are the perfect greeting as guests sit down at the table for tea and cake. Your company feels pampered and special because someone has gone to all this effort. Slow down and enjoy the company over a cup of hot tea.

TIP » Use clothespins to hold trimmings in place until the glue dries.

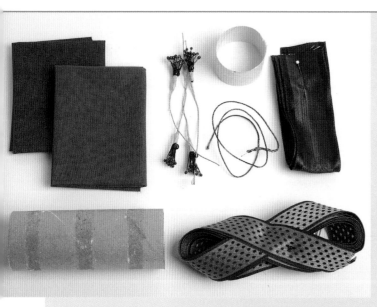

Materials (for 4)

Solid cotton fabric in fuchsia and green
Embroidery floss: 1 skein each of Presencia #5075, #9860, #2419, #2397, #2402, and #2415
#1 punchneedle
28-gauge green floral wire
32-gauge white wire, colored magenta
4 black pearl stamens
Green floral tape
Cardboard paper towel roll, cut into 1" pieces
3 yd. decorative wire-edged ribbon, 1" wide (four 7" pieces and four 18" pieces)
⅞ yd. solid-color ribbon, 1½" wide (four 7" pieces)
Seam sealant
Embellishing glue
Small paintbrush
Fabric glue
Spring-type clothespins

See chapter 2 for more information on fabric, glue, colored wire, and other materials.

Patterns

petal   **leaf**

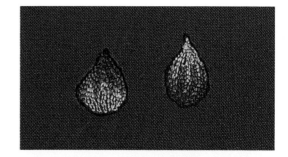

Directions

1. Trace five petals for each flower onto the fuchsia fabric (20 total). Trace five leaves for each flower stem onto the green fabric (20 total).

2. Using one strand of embroidery floss in the #1 needle, outline all the petals with #2419. Work some petals from light to dark, using #2397 as the lightest shade, #2402 as the medium shade, and #2415 as the dark shade. Keep the transitions between colors irregular for a more interesting color change. Work other petals from dark to light. Mixing the two petal variations in one flower makes it more interesting. Outline the leaves with #5075 and fill them in with #9860.

3. Seal all the edges of the petals and leaves with seam sealant. Let dry. Repeat.

4. Lightly coat the back of each piece with embellishing glue. Let dry.

5. Cut out each piece as close as possible to the embroidery. Using embellishing glue, glue a 3" length of 28-gauge green wire to the back of each leaf. Glue a 3" length of 32-gauge magenta wire to the back of each petal.

6. Make four sets of three leaves joined together with floral tape. Make the remaining eight leaves into four sets of two leaves each, again joined together with floral tape. Evenly space each set of five petals around a stamen and wrap with floral tape. Make sure to use both petal coloring variations in each flower. Add a three-leaf set and a two-leaf set to each flower using floral tape. Cover any remaining exposed wire with floral tape. Curl each stem around a pencil to shape it.

7. Line the inside of each cardboard tube segment with the 1½" wide ribbon, folding under the raw edges. Glue with fabric glue. Fold the ¼" overhang on each side of the ring to the outside of the cardboard to cover the raw edge of the tube. Glue in place.

8. Remove the wire from the edges of the 7" lengths of 1" wide decorative ribbon. Matching the seams of the lining ribbon, cover the outside of each section of cardboard tube, turn under the raw edge at the end, and glue in place with fabric glue.

9. Attach a flower to the top of each napkin ring, over the seam, using fabric glue. Hold in place with a clothespin until dry. Tie the 18" length of wired ribbon around the cardboard, over the seams and the flower stem. Tie in a bow. Trim the ends in a V and "fluff" the bows to finish.

Bluebells on a Quilt Block Pillow

Materials

16½" square quilt block, new or vintage
Fabric for back of pillow, two pieces
    12 by 16½"
Embroidery floss—1 skein each of #5075,
    #9850, #3411, #3387, #3396, and #3400
#1 punchneedle
16" square pillow form
2 yards coordinating piping with a flange
    (or enough to go around pillow)
Hand sewing thread
White iron-on nylon tricot interfacing
Iron-on transfer pencil
Tracing paper
Iron
White or silver fabric pencil
Sewing machine with zipper foot attachment
Embroidery needle

See chapter 2 for more information on fabric, glue, colored wire, and other materials.

Bluebells thrive in the English woods. They are one of the earliest flowers to bloom in spring, following crocus and snowdrops. Soon the forest floor is carpeted with delicate stalks, each laden with tiny, bell-shaped flowers. I've only seen photographs of a bluebell wood, but in spring our Texas fields of bluebonnets evoke a similar response.

    These bluebells needed a special background— and I found it in a vintage quilt block. This block is unusual because of its size (over 16" square), fabric (lightweight wool), and colors (oatmeal, magenta, and blue). The blue center of the block complements the colors of bluebells. It's a perfect marriage. One day I'll add a blue butterfly pin or two (from project 9, page 50) to the pillow.

Pattern

Pattern shown at 90%.
Enlarge by 10% or as
needed to fit your pillow.

TIP ›› I strongly recommend you use a padded embroidery hoop for this project if you are using a vintage quilt block. Even if your entire embroidered design fits inside the hoop, the background is very delicate and deserves the extra protection a padded hoop can give.

Directions

1. Following the manufacturer's directions, iron the nylon tricot interfacing to the back of the quilt block.

2. Trace the bluebell pattern onto tracing paper with the iron-on transfer pencil. Place the image right side down on the nylon tricot. Hold the hot iron in place on the pattern until the pattern is transferred. Do not slide the iron back and forth over the pattern. This can cause the pattern to shift, blurring the design lines.

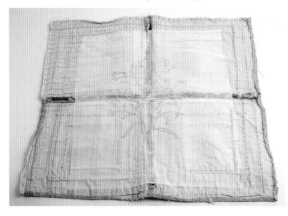

3. Before starting the embroidery, work a small test area in an inconspicuous part of the fabric to see if the loop height needs to be adjusted. In my case, it did: Because of the heavier fabric, the seam allowances in the patchwork, and the extra layer of the nylon tricot, I had to add ⅛" to my needle shaft in order to get a good loop on the right side of the pillow. If needed, adjust your needle, following the manufacturer's directions, before proceeding.

4. Outline the leaves with #5075 and fill them in with #9850. Outline the flower petals, details, and buds with #3411. Fill in the petals, using #3400 on the lower portions of the petals, #3396 in the middle, and #3387 for the highlights and the tips of the petals.

5. Referring to the pattern, draw in the stems freehand on the right side of the block with the silver or white fabric pencil. With three strands of #9850 in an embroidery needle, embroider the flower stems on the front of the block in stem stitch.

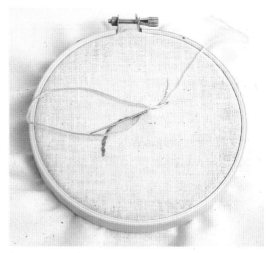

Stem stitch—front.

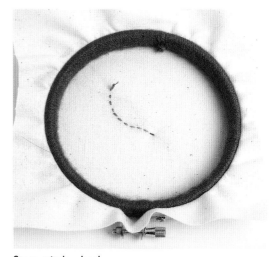

Stem stitch—back.

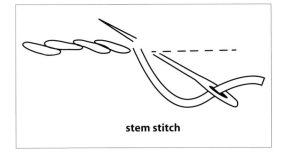

stem stitch

6. Pin the piping around all sides of the quilt block on the right side, aligning the raw edges of the flange and the pillow top, with the piping on the inside. Baste the piping to the pillow top by hand, using thread in a contrasting color. Clip the flange at the corners. Overlap the raw edges of the piping at the end and tuck them into the seam allowance. Set aside.

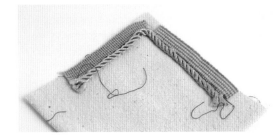

7. Turn under a ¼" hem on one long (16½") side of each backing piece. Press. Turn under an additional ¼" and stitch close to the edge.

TIP » Using a contrasting color for the basting thread makes it easier to see. Machine stitch between the basting and the piping for a clean finish.

8. With right sides together, place the backing pieces on top of the pillow top. The hemmed edges of the backing pieces will overlap in the middle to make a lapped back. Align all raw edges of the front and back. Stitch around all four sides, as close to the piping as possible for a clean edge. Using a zipper foot attachment on the sewing machine allows you to get even closer. Slightly round the corners for easier stitching.

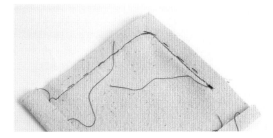

9. Trim the corners, then turn the pillow right side out. Lightly steam the edges for a crisp edge before inserting the pillow form.

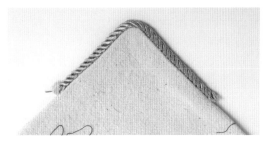

PROJECT 20
A Pair of
Framed Poppies

This pair of framed poppies started with the red poppy on the yellow silk. For the companion piece, rather than embroidering a different flower, I decided to show the difference when the same design is worked in another color combination. One flower is worked in warm colors and the other in cool colors. The leaves on both flowers are the same color, but they look different against different background colors. The two flowers use several different punchneedle techniques and needle sizes. Beads and traditional hand embroidery stitches give additional visual interest and texture.

The background fabric used in these projects is dupioni silk, an unexpected fabric choice for punchneedle. Its sheen and color add elegance to the overall project.

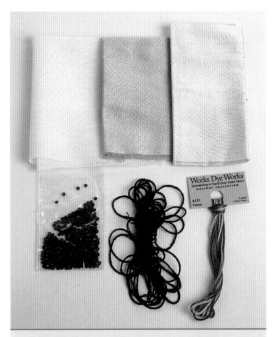

Materials

Two 10 by 12" squares of background fabric
of choice (silk, linen, or cotton)
White nylon tricot fusible interfacing
Tracing paper
Iron-on transfer pencil
Iron
#1 and #3 punchneedles
Black faceted seed beads
Beading needle and black sewing thread
Embroidery floss—see box, above right
2 picture frames

*See chapter 2 for more information on fabric, glue,
colored wire, and other materials.*

EMBROIDERY FLOSS COLORS USED FOR THIS PROJECT

Leaves: Presencia #5084, #9865, and #5156
Red poppy: Presencia #2171, #1902, #0007,
    #4723, and #4812; Weeks Dye Works
    #4131, "Fiesta"
Magenta poppy: Presencia #2419, #2394,
    #2406, #2402, #2397, #4805, and #2595
Blue butterfly: Presencia #3223, #1140,
    #1000, #8083, and #8779
Yellow butterfly: Presencia #7580, #8083,
    #1152, #1062, and #1232
Both poppies: Black rayon embroidery floss

Directions:

1. Following the manufacturer's directions, trace
the design onto the tracing paper using an iron-
on transfer pencil.
2. Iron nylon tricot fusible interfacing to the wrong
side of the background fabric (if using silk or another delicate fabric).
3. Place the iron-on transfer on the nylon tricot,
right side down, centering the design on the
fabric. Hold the hot iron in place over one part
of the design at a time until the pattern is transferred to the tricot. When moving to another
part of the design lift the iron completely off the
paper. Do not slide the iron back and forth over
the pattern; this can cause the image to shift
and the design to blur. If you are making two
poppies, you should be able to use the same
transfer again for the second image.

TIP » Pin the design in place before transferring
the image. This can reduce the chances of the pattern shifting while you transfer it.

4. Using two strands of embroidery floss in a #3
needle, outline the leaves, stems, and bud with
#5084. Fill in the leaves and bud with #9865.
For a seamless transition of color, start a new
piece of the variegated thread with the same
color as the end of the previous piece (light to
light, dark to dark). Fill in the stems with #5156.

Pattern

5. For the petals, use two strands of floss in a #3 needle throughout.

   Red poppy: Outline the flower and bud with #2171. Work the folded-over parts of the bud and petal with #1902, and the bases of the petals with #0007. Fill in the rest of the petals with Weeks Dye Works #4131, Fiesta.

   Magenta poppy: Outline the flower and bud with #2419. Work the folded-over parts of the bud and petal with #2394. Work the petals with #2406 for the shadows and the bases of the petals, #2402 for the middles of the petals, and #2397 for the lightest parts at the tops of the petals.

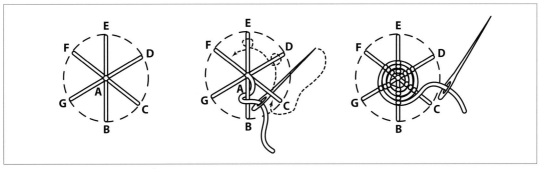

Ribbed spider web stitch.

6. The centers of the poppies are embroidered with a ribbed spider web stitch. Using a hand sewing needle and black rayon thread, lay out the spokes of the spider web in the center of the poppy, going up at A and down at B, then up again at A and down at C, then up at A and down at D, and so on all the way around. Then come up again at A and wrap the thread around spoke B, then around spoke C, and so on. Continue around in a spiral, wrapping the spokes until the center area is covered. Tie off the thread at the back of the work.

7. For the outer ring of the centers, reset the gauge or stopper on your needle to add ¼" to the distance between the needle's eye and the gauge or stopper. For the red poppy, work two rows of

#4723 right next to the petals. Fill in the rest of the area up to the spider web center (approximately two rows of stitches) with #4812. For the magenta poppy, work the outer two rows in #2595 and fill in with #4805.

8. For the butterfly, change to the #1 punchneedle and work with one strand of embroidery floss throughout.

   Blue butterfly: Outline the butterfly with #8779. Work the outsides of the wings with #3223, the middle parts of the wings with #1000, and the inner upper wing with #1140.

   Yellow butterfly: Outline the butterfly with #7580. Work the outsides of the wings with #1152, the middle parts of the wings with #1062, and the inner upper wing with #1232.

9. For the bodies of the butterflies, reset the gauge or stopper on your needle to add a shallow ¼". Work each body densely in #8083. Clip the loops to create a velvet texture, then sculpt the body.

10. Return the gauge or stopper on the needle to its original setting. From the front, work the antennae with curving lines of #8083, punching loops from the front to the back to create reverse punchneedle stitches.

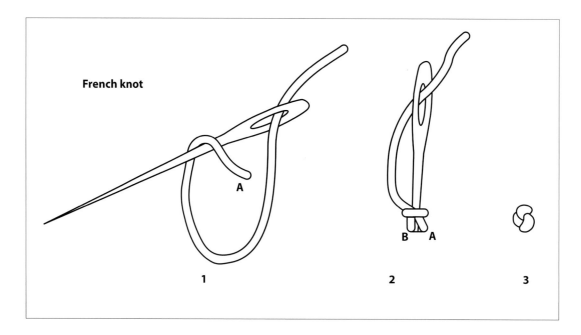

French knot

A

B   A

1   2   3

11. With a threaded hand sewing needle and one strand of #8083, make a tiny French knot—wrapping the thread around the needle only once—at the end of each antenna from the front.

12. Using one strand of black rayon thread, work a long stitch from the spider web center out into the petals for a stamen. Make at least three stamens in each petal.

13. Using a beading needle and black sewing thread, sew one seed bead at the end of each stamen. Sew a small cluster of beads in the center of the spider web stitch.

14. Using one strand of #5156 and a hand sewing needle, make small, irregular straight stitches at right angles up both sides of each stem to create small "hairs" along the stem.

15. Mount and frame the embroidery as desired.

VARIATION

French knots made with black rayon thread may be substituted for the beads on the stamens if desired.

TIP Use acid-free or archival backing when framing. This protects the embroidery from potential deterioration.

Bowl of Pansies

Pansies have a number of romantic and whimsical names: heartsease, tittle-my-fancy, kiss-me-at-the-garden-gate, and love-in-idleness. The name "pansy" is derived from *pensée,* the French word for "thought." The pansy stands for remembrance in the Victorian language of flowers. It's hard to see a pansy and not smile.

I wanted my embroidered pansies to be as real-looking as possible, and I'm happy with the results. As I made the individual flowers for this arrange-

ment, I discovered that the more I made, the prettier the arrangement became. This was obviously a labor of love because there are 17 pansies!

All the pansies are constructed the same way; the only difference between them is the colors used. So I've given a single set of directions for making one flower, which can be used for any color combination you choose. The specific colors of floss to use for each color combination are listed separately. If you're up for it, make a whole bowlful!

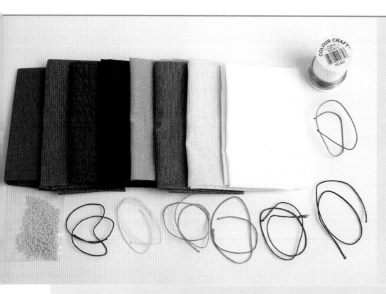

Materials

Solid cotton fabric in green and assorted colors

Embroidery floss: 1 skein each of Presencia #4485 and #4817 for all leaves (See color list for colors used for each flower)

#1 punchneedle

28-gauge green floral wire

32-gauge white floral wire, colored to match petals

20-gauge green floral wire

Yellow seed beads (3 per flower)

Green floral tape

Fine spool wire

Seam sealant

Embellishing glue

Small paintbrush

OPTIONAL: Vase or container, dry floral foam, and sheet moss for the arrangement.

See chapter 2 for more information on fabric, glue, colored wire, and other materials.

Patterns

pansy petal patterns

make one of each petal
per flower

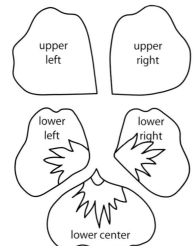

pansy leaves

Add 1–3 assorted leaves
to each pansy stem

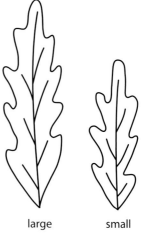

White Pansy (make 3): Background fabric, white cotton; outline and veins, #8400; main petal color, #1000; face outline, #0007; face, #2720; center, #1134 .

Yellow Pansy (make 1): Background fabric, yellow cotton; outline and veins, #1109; main petal color, #1098; face, #8083; center, #1000.

Lavender Pansy (make 3): Background fabric, lavender cotton; outline and veins, #3073; main petal color, #2705; face, #2595; center, #1000.

COLOR SCHEMES

Here are the color combinations I used in my arrangement:

Dark Purple Pansy (make 2): Background fabric, purple cotton; outline and veins #3327; upper petal main color, #2711; lower petal main color, #9500; face, #0007; center, #1134.

Two-Tone Lavender Pansy (make 3, 1 with dark upper petals and light lower petals, and 2 with light upper petals and dark lower petals): Background fabric, light and dark lavender cotton; outline and veins, #3073; main petal color, #2705 and #2699; face, #2595; center, #1000.

Yellow and Purple Pansy (make 3): Background fabric, yellow and purple cotton; lower petal outline and veins, #1109; lower petal main color, #1098; upper petal outline and veins, #3327; upper petal main color, #2635; face, #8083; center #1000.

Yellow and Rust Pansy (make 2): Background fabric, yellow and rust cotton; lower petal outline and veins, #2171; lower petal main color, #7492; upper petal outline and veins, #1109; upper petal main color, #1098; face, #8083; center, #1000.

Directions

1. For each flower, trace one lower center petal, two lower side petals (left and right), and two upper petals (left and right) on the background fabric. Draw the veins on each of the petals and the "face" on the center petal freehand, using the pattern as a reference. Drawing these features freehand adds individuality to the flowers; no two are absolutely identical.

**pansy petal
veins and face**

TIP » Since I was making a lot of flowers, I first made plastic templates of the petal and leaf pieces. It made all that tracing go a little easier and quicker!

2. Outline the petals and embroider the veins in the darkest color. Fill in with the main petal color. Embroider the face on the lower petals with the designated color; run some of the face stitches into the main petal color for a more realistic look. Work the very innermost tip at the center of each lower petal with white or pale yellow for the center.

3. Trace one or two leaves for each flower on the green cotton, using a mixture of large and small leaves. Outline the leaves and work the veins with #4485. Fill in with #4817.

4. Seal all petals and leaves with seam sealant. Let dry. Repeat.

5. Lightly coat the backs of all petals and leaves with embellishing glue. Let dry.

6. Cut out each piece as close as possible to the embroidery. If making more than one color pansy at a time, take care not to mix up the petals of the different flowers.

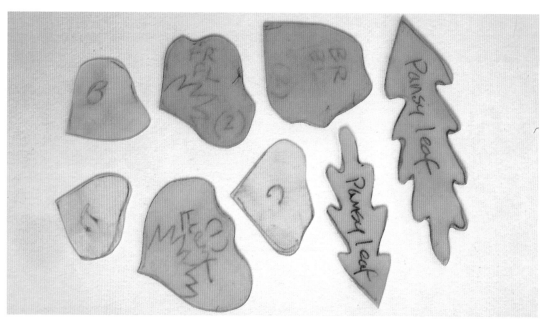

My templates in two sizes—the large versions were used for this project, but you could reduce the patterns and make some lovely miniature pansies as well.

7. Use embellishing glue to glue a piece of 28-gauge green floral wire cut 1" longer than the leaf onto the back of each leaf. Wrap a 3½ to 4" piece of 32-gauge floral wire, colored to match the petals, around your finger to form a loop. Glue a loop of wire to the back of each petal with embellishing glue, shaping it to fit inside the edge.

8. Thread three seed beads onto a 4" piece of fine wire. Fold the wire in half with beads in the middle. Twist the wire tightly to gather the three beads into a cluster for the stamen.

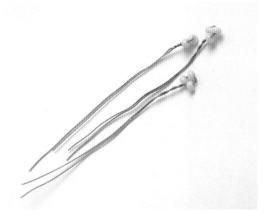

9. Arrange one lower center petal tight against the beaded stamen, and wrap with floral tape. Add a lower right and lower left petal on the sides, slightly behind the center petal, and wrap with floral tape, then add an upper right and upper left petal, again wrapping with tape to secure. Attach the finished flower to a 4 to 6" 20-gauge green wire stem with floral tape. Add one or two leaves to the stem as desired.

10. Carefully shape each petal with your fingers to give the pansy a realistic look. Gently curl each leaf away from the stem.

11. Place a piece of dry floral foam in your vase or bowl and cover it with a piece of sheet moss. Arrange the pansies in the foam as desired.

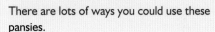

VARIATIONS

There are lots of ways you could use these pansies.
- Group two or three together on a pin for a jacket or hat.
- Tie one to a gift for an extra treat.
- Use on napkin rings like the ones on page 73.
- Arrange four or five in a teacup.
- Add to a piece of flat embroidery for extra dimension.

Miniature Purple Iris

There are over 300 species of iris. This one is a German or bearded iris in miniature. The top petals are called "stands" because they stand upright, while the bottom petals with the "beards" are called "falls." The genus was named "iris" for the rainbow, because the flowers come in so many colors. Check out a bulb catalog for photos of different varieties and color combinations. A selection of irises in various colors in a vase (like the bowl of pansies on page 85) would make an impressive display. Or you can do as I did and display just a couple of these tiny flowers in a vintage perfume bottle.

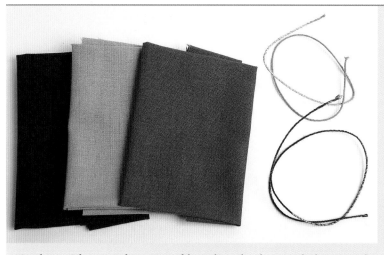

See chapter 2 for more information on fabric, glue, colored wire, and other materials.

Materials

Solid cotton fabric in lavender, purple, and green
Embroidery floss: 1 skein each of Presencia #5084, #9865, #2595, #2635, #2627, #2615, and #1227
#3 punchneedle
20-gauge green floral wire
28-gauge green floral wire
32-gauge white floral wire, colored to match petals
Green floral tape
Seam sealant
Embellishing glue
Small paintbrush
Silver or white fabric pencil

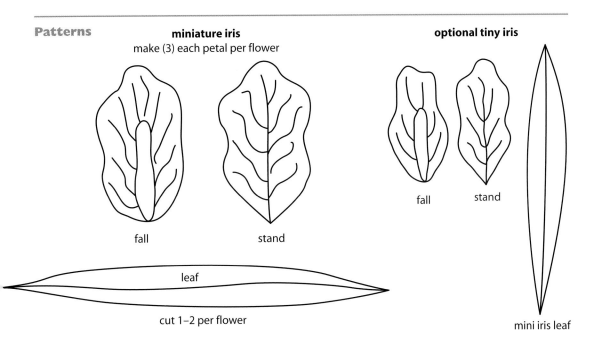

Patterns

miniature iris
make (3) each petal per flower

fall   stand

leaf
cut 1–2 per flower

optional tiny iris

fall   stand

mini iris leaf

Directions

1. With a white or silver fabric pencil, trace three stands for each flower onto the lavender fabric; and trace three falls for each flower onto the purple fabric. Draw the veins on each of the six petals freehand, using the illustration for reference. Leave room for the beard in the center of each fall. Trace one or two leaves for each flower onto the green fabric.

2. Using two strands of embroidery floss in a #3 needle throughout, outline the stands and work their veins in #2595; fill in each stand with #2635. For the falls, outline the petals and work the veins with #2627, and fill in with #2615.

3. For the beards, reset the gauge or stopper on the needle to add ¼" to the distance between the needle's eye and the gauge or stopper. Densely work the beard area with #1227. Clip the tops of the loops to create a velvet texture.

4. Reset the gauge to its original position and outline each leaf with #5084, then fill in with #9865. Start each new length of varie-

gated floss with the last color of the previous piece for a seamless transition (light to light, dark to dark).

5. Seal the edges of all the pieces with seam sealant. Let dry. Repeat.

6. Lightly cover the back of each piece with a coat of embellishing glue. Let dry.

7. Cut out all pieces as close as possible to the embroidery. Sculpt the beards into rounded shapes. Leave the center areas high, and trim the sides of each beard close to the height of the surrounding loops.

8. Glue a 5 to 6" piece of 28-gauge wire to the back of each leaf with embellishing glue. Glue a 5½ to 6½" length of 32-gauge lavender wire shaped to fit inside the edge of the petal to each fall. Do the same for the stands with purple wire.

9. Attach the three stands to the top of a 6 to 8" length of 20-gauge wire with floral tape. Make sure the wire faces the inside on each stand. Add the falls between the stands, facing downward, and attach them to the stem with floral tape. Add one or two leaves to the stem and cover the entire stem with floral tape.

10. Arrange in a container for display.

Miniature Flame Tulips

Materials

Solid cotton fabric in red and green
Embroidery floss: 1 skein each of Presencia
    #4485, #5400, #9060, #1166, and #1667
#1 punchneedle
20-gauge green floral wire
28-gauge green floral wire
32-gauge white floral wire, colored red
Green floral tape
Seam sealant
Embellishing glue
Small paintbrush

See chapter 2 for more information on fabric, glue, colored wire, and other materials.

Is there a happier sight than brightly colored tulips in spring? It's easy to understand why Europeans were obsessed with these flowers in the 1600s, when they were first introduced to Europe from Turkey.

Tulips come in a riot of colors, including many bicolored ones. I love the red and yellow variety called "Flame." These are miniatures—the tulip head is just over 1" tall. They look charming in

a little *tulipière* (that's French for "special tulip vase"). If you'd like to make larger flowers, you can enlarge the pattern with a copy machine. For other color options, refer to a tulip bulb catalog for inspiration. You'll be amazed at the variety.

Patterns

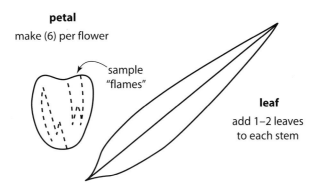

petal

make (6) per flower

sample "flames"

leaf

add 1–2 leaves to each stem

Directions

1. To make three flowers, trace three sets of six petals (18 petals in all) onto the red cotton. Trace four leaves onto the green cotton.

2. Using one strand of #1667, outline each tulip petal. Using one strand of #9060, randomly work vertical "flames"; it's best if each petal is different from the others. Refer to the photos and illustration for examples. Fill in the remaining areas with one strand of #1166.

3. Outline the leaves and work the veins with #4485. Fill in with #5400.

4. Seal all the edges of the pieces with seam sealant. Let dry. Repeat.

5. Lightly cover the back of each piece with a thin coat of embellishing glue. Let dry.

6. Cut out all the pieces as close as possible to the embroidery. Bend a 4" piece of 32-gauge red wire around your fingertip to form a loop in the shape of a petal. Using embellishing glue, glue the loop onto the back of a petal. Repeat with the other 17 petals. Glue a 5½ to 6" length of 28-gauge wire to the center of the back of each leaf. Let all the pieces dry.

7. Put three petals together with the wire facing inside and wrap with floral tape. Add three more petals around the first three, wire side in, evenly spacing them to cover any gaps. Attach the tulip head to a 4 to 6" length of 20-gauge wire with floral tape. Repeat for the other two flowers.

8. Using floral tape, attach two leaves to one tulip stem and one leaf each to the remaining two stems.

9. Arrange in a container for display.

Gallery

All of the pieces in the Gallery were designed and made by the author.

*Peacock feathers were embroidered on raw tussah silk with a #3 needle.
Metallic threads add iridescence to the feathers. I finished the piece into
a pillow using hand-dyed silk velvet and brocade ribbon.*

This monarch butterfly was embroidered on raw
tussah silk using both #1 and #3 needles. The branch
is stitched with blended threads to achieve a realistic
look. A number of variegated threads capture the
brilliant colors of autumn leaves.

This rainbow trout was embroidered with a #3 needle on a background of wool suiting. I used thread blending to capture the subtle rainbow coloring on the side of the fish. A glass bead for the eye and variegated metallic thread scattered on the back of the fish give the piece extra sparkle. It is mounted on an empty cigar box. It's a new kind of "green" trophy fish.

The feather embroidery in the inset on the handbag
has clipped-loop velvet accents. The background
fabric was machine quilted, then embroidered with
a #3 needle. I worked the feather in greater detail
with a #1 needle to create the subtle shading.

Many techniques were used in this small wall quilt. The background is hand-dyed, -stamped, and -stitched paper, accented with velvet and painted Tyvek leaves. Three-dimensional fabric branches with wired punchneedle leaves add depth, along with a small bird, a handmade lizard pin, and a tin butterfly pin tucked into the branches.

This multi-level wall quilt is embellished with three-dimensional punchneedle embroidery. The sky quilt behind the window is free motion–quilted, with painted birds, and the middle background is a pieced quilt. The front quilt is a photo transfer collage. Three-dimensional rocks, an open door, and a fabric tree covered with individual punchneedle leaves add more layers to the piece. I worked the punchneedle leaves and flowers with a #3 needle, with blended thread colors in the petals of the day lily and variegated thread in the leaves. From the collection of Simplicity Creative Group.

This stylized sunflower is stitched with hand-dyed #5 perle cotton thread in a #6 punchneedle, and the background is hand-dyed Weaver's Cloth (both from Weeks Dye Works). I outlined the small embroidery with piping and appliquéd it off-center on a pillow.

Embroidery Floss Conversion Chart

Presencia	DMC	Anchor	Presencia	DMC	Anchor	Presencia	DMC	Anchor
0007	310	403	2402	3607	87	5075	520	263
1000	BLANC	2	2406	718	88	5084	934	1044
1062	743	302	2415	917	89	5156	3363	860
1068	742	307	2419	915	1028	5400	732	280
1094	727	293	2595	154	72	7471	922	1003
1098	726	297	2615	3827	97	7475	921	339
1109	783	308	2627	552	99	7492	920	341
1134	677	292	2635	327	100	7567	721	326
1140	725	303	2699	155	110	7580	900	340
1152	741	314	2705	3746	1030	7825	3857	351
1166	666	46	2711	333	111	8032	3860	354
1227	444	291	2720	550	101	8072	434	309
1232	972	303	2732	159	117	8075	433	310
1237	740	324	3068	158	940	8080	898	360
1314	352	328	3073	791	119	8083	3371	380
1325	3340	329	3223	3755	977	8400	644	830
1490	817	13	3327	823	150	8705	317	400
1667	150	59	3387	157	130	8756	3799	401
1889	3706	33	3396	799	136	8779	318	399
1895	891	35	3400	3838	131	8785	414	235
1902	321	9046	3411	797	134	9060	90	1217
1906	498	1005	3822	995	1089	9100	108	1220
1915	815	43	4485	895	218			(darker)
2171	902	45	4561	988	817	9350	112	1201
2314	604	74	4565	3345	269	9395	48	1204
2323	3806	52	4723	907	255	9500	52	1209
2333	3804	63	4799	472	253			(lighter)
2390	153	73	4805	166	279	9850	92	1216
2394	3609	85	4812	581	280	9860	122	1215
2397	3608	86	4817	580	266	9865	94	1216

Resources

Punchneedles

Bernadine's Needle Art
Phone: 888-884-8576
Fax: 217-543-2996
Website: http://www.bernadinesneedleart.com
Punchneedles, threads, silk ribbons, patterns, kits, and books.

Birdhouse Enterprises/Igolochkoy
Phone: 916-452-5212
Fax: 916-452-1212
Website: http://www.gailbird.com
E-mail: gail@gailbird.com
Igolochkoy punchneedles, kits, patterns, punch-needle certification program.

Clover Needlecraft, Inc.
Phone: 800-233-1703
Fax: 562-282-0220
Website: http://www.clover-usa.com
E-mail: customercare@clover-usa.com
Punchneedles, hoops, threads, iron-on transfer pencils, clam shell accessory case, other sewing notions and tools.

The Punchneedle Marketplace
Phone: 800-272-1966 or 269-471-1111
Website: http://www.punchneedlemarketplace.com
Many brands of punchneedles, patterns, books, hoops, fabric, acrylic yarn; certified instructor list available.

Several of the projects in this book use purchased bags, boxes, and more. These projects can be adapted to work with many different products, but if you want to use the same ones I did, look for these items:

- The Tiger Lily Jewelry Box (project 11): item #BAG 38 F (Jewelry Case) from Lee's Needle Art Leather Goods.
- The Clam Shell Coin Purse (project 15): item #8411 (Clam Shell Accessories Case Medium) from Clover Needlecraft, Inc.
- The Embroidered Inset Handbag (project 16): item #BAG47 (Classic Bag) from Lee's Needle Art Leather Goods.
- The Stargazer Lily Tote Bag (project 17): item #BAG26 (Nylon Tote Bag, 15" W x 11" H x 6" D) from Lee's Needle Art Leather Goods.

Thread, Fabric, and Other Sewing Goods

Colonial Needle Co.
Phone: 800-963-3353
Fax: 914-946-7002
Website: http://www.colonialneedle.com
E-mail: terry@colonialneedle.com
Presencia embroidery floss, hoops, Lee's Needle Art Leather Goods (bags, cases, and more).

Michael Miller Fabrics LLC.
Phone: 212-704-0774
Fax: 212-633-0272
Website: http://www.michaelmillerfabrics.com
E-mail: info@michaelmillerfabrics.com
All the cotton fabrics used in the projects in this book are from this company. They offer Cotton Couture—a high-quality solid-color cotton fabric—as well as many prints.

Weeks Dye Works
Phone: 877-OVERDYE (877-683-7393)
Fax: 919-772-8757
Website: http://www.weeksdyeworks.com
E-mail: contact@weeksdyeworks.com
Hand-dyed six-strand cotton embroidery floss, perle cotton, hand-dyed Weaver's Cloth, over-dyed wool fabric.

Miscellaneous Supplies

Beacon Adhesives
Phone: 914-699-3400
Fax: 914-699-2783
Website: http://www.beaconcreates.com
E-mail: beaconadheasives@yahoo.com
Fabri-Tac fabric glue, Gem-Tac embellishing glue, Quick-Grip all-purpose adhesive.

Sulky of America, Inc.
Phone: 800-874-4115 or 770-429-3973
Fax: 770-429-3987
Website: http://www.sulky.com
E-mail: asksulky@sulky.com
Iron-on transfer pens in eight colors and white, threads (including metallic), iron-on nylon tricot fusible interfacing, books.

Prym Consumer USA, Inc.
Phone: 800-845-4948
Fax: 864-587-3322
E-mail: laura.mooney@prym-consumer-usa.com
Fray-Check seam sealant, other sewing products.

General Craft Suppliers

Fabric, embroidery floss, jewelry findings, glues, and more.

A. C. Moore
Phone: 888-ACMOORE
Website: http://www.acmoore.com

Hancock Fabrics
Website: http://www.hancockfabrics.com

Hobby Lobby
Website: http://www.hobbylobby.com

Jo-Ann Fabric and Craft Stores
Phone: 888-739-4120
Fax: 330-463-6760
Website: http://www.joann.com

Michaels
Phone: 800-MICHAELS (800-642-4235)
Website: http://www.michaels.com/

Books

Punchneedle: The Complete Guide
by Marinda Stewart
Published by Krause Publications